The
Fast Forward
Mindset

David Schnurman

Author's Note

Writing this book, I have relied on journals, texts, emails, the memories of friends and colleagues, and my own recollections. In places I have changed the names of individuals in order to protect their privacy, or have compressed the chronology of events in order to ensure easy, informative reading and clarity. I created the dialog in this book from memory, but have strived to make it as close as possible to what actually was said at the time. Overall, I have made an effort to assure that everything written in this book is accurate and truthful. The views expressed are my personal opinions.

ENTREPRENEUR EDITION

THE
FAST FORWARD
MINDSET

How to be Fearless & Focused to Accelerate Your Success

DAVID SCHNURMAN

WWW.HIGHPOINTPUBS.COM

This edition published by Highpoint Executive Publishing. For information, write to info@highpointpubs.com.

First Edition

ISBN: 978-1-64570-879-7

Library of Congress Cataloging-in-Publication Data

Schnurman, David
The Fast Forward Mindset: How to Be Fearless & Focused to Accelerate Your Success

Includes index.

Summary: "Author David Schnurman reveals the challenges, fears, exhilaration, and hard-won lessons he learned in founding and growing his award-wining company, Lawline – resulting in a set of simple, yet powerful tools that you can apply to your own entrepreneur's journey." – Provided by publisher.

ISBN: 978-1-64570-879-7 (softcover)
1. Entrepreneurship 2. Self-Improvement

Library of Congress Control Number: 2019937220

Book Design by Sarah Clarehart
Cover Design by Damian Makki

Manufactured in the United States of America

10 9 8 7 6 5 4 3 2 1

PRAISE FOR
THE FAST FORWARD MINDSET

"*The Fast Forward Mindset* does a great job in showing you the journey of an entrepreneur through different stages of business and leadership growth. David Schnurman's memorable stories and practices will quickly put you on your own path of success."

– VERNE HARNISH, Founder Entrepreneurs' Organization (EO) and author of *Scaling Up (Rockefeller Habits 2.0)*

"Having worked with thousands of entrepreneurs over the years, I can tell you that David's stories are the exact struggles I see leaders go through day-in and day-out. *The Fast Forward Mindset* provides you with guidance on how to not only survive, but thrive in this environment."

– GINO WICKMAN, author of *Traction* and creator of EOS

"In *The Fast Forward Mindset*, David distilled his own experiences into a powerful three-step formula that will help you break through any barrier in your way. If you're ready to become a fearless and focused leader, David's book shows you how."

– MIKE MICHALOWICZ, bestselling author of *Profit First, Clockwork* and *The Pumpkin Plan*

"If you want to be a successful entrepreneur, this book is a must-read. Open it up, follow the plan, practice the mindset, then go out and make your impact on the world. Your roadmap is right here."

– DAVE KERPEN, chairman, Likeable; and *New York Times* bestselling author of *Likeable Social Media* and *The Art of People*

"For entrepreneurs looking to accelerate their business and success, *The Fast Forward Mindset* is THE book to read this year. You will learn the steps you need to get out of your comfort zone so you can break through your mental walls!"

– RYAN AVERY, international keynote speaker

CONTENTS

FOREWORD

I met David in 2013 after he read *The Miracle Morning: The Not-So-Obvious Secret to Transform Your Life Before 8AM*. He shared his passion for my book, but most importantly he said he wanted to help me spread the message to increase the impact you have on the world.

He took action right away by joining a weekly call to brainstorm ways to spread my message. He took more action the next year by inviting me to Entrepreneurs Organization in New York to share my story. He then hosted an event in his office and convinced me to film it and put it on YouTube to reach a larger audience. It is a good thing he did too, as that video now has over half a million views.

Over the years, David has kept his commitment to support me and *The Miracle Morning mission: Elevating the Consciousness of Humanity, One Morning at a Time*. In fact, spreading the power of entrepreneurship can be seen throughout his career. From starting a cable television show interviewing top entrepreneurs, to becoming chapter president of Entrepreneurs Organization in New York, his goal has always been to help others grow in their life and their business.

The way David has shown up for me is how he is with everything in his life. Watching what David has built with Lawline has been nothing short of inspiring. His company has both an award-winning culture and an unparalleled learning platform, allowing it to have a significant impact on the legal community. In addition, he is constantly practicing what he preaches by working with coaches, mentors, and peers to improve his skills as a leader and entrepreneur.

This book embodies everything that David is as a person, and is his ultimate contribution to the entrepreneur community at large. And in true fashion, he does not do it by showing off all of his proudest moments, but by honestly revealing some of his more challenging mental roadblocks and how he got through them.

Even with his personal and entrepreneurial stories throughout, David makes it clear that the book is not about him, but about you, the reader. How can you live your life fearlessly and more focused? How you can step outside of your comfort zone more often to grow as an individual? Since he is an admitted self-help addict, he has read hundreds of books on entrepreneurship and mindset. One thing is clear as a result: He learned how to write a killer business and self-improvement book.

The Fast Forward Mindset is both inspirational and practical. It has just the right amount of mindset techniques mixed with personal stories to keep you engaged along the way. Most importantly, David organizes his approach into the following three steps: 1) Take Action, 2) NIP Fear in the Bud, and 3) Find Your Focus. This makes it easy to know what to do the moment you finish the book. Lastly, it is only a three-hour read which allows you to go right from reading the book to implementing those three steps within a short period of time.

You are in for a treat. Once you read *The Fast Forward Mindset*, there is no going back. So sit back, relax, and get reading!

Sincerely,

Hal Elrod
International bestselling author of *The Miracle Morning, The Miracle Equation, & The Miracle Morning Series*

DEDICATION

This book is dedicated to my three wonderful children Leila, Joshua, and Jonah. It was written with you three in mind, as I hope someday you will take the time to read it to help you on your own life's journey. To my wife, Kelli, who is everything to me and challenges me in all the right ways. I love you more each day. And finally, to my parents, Judy & Alan, who raised me to put family first. Your love for each other has been such an inspiration.

INTRODUCTION

 *5 Minutes*

If you are like me, you are proud of who you are and what you have achieved in your life, yet there is a voice inside your head that says you should be further along than you are right now. That voice usually focuses on 1) things you always expected to do and achieve, and 2) the impact you expected to have on others. This book allows you to answer that voice and fast-forward the entrepreneurial impact you are meant to have on the world around you.

Within five years, beginning in 2006, I took my company, Lawline, from $0 in revenue to $5 million. Now, in 2019, it is one of the largest national providers of online continuing legal education (CLE) with over 130,000 attorneys who've completed more than three million courses on our website and apps! We have always understood the need that exists in the market and we know how to serve it right.

It was not always this way. Early on, we were ignored by the major bar associations and large national providers. As we grew, we often were dismissed because of our lower price. Whenever we would attend industry conferences, you could hear murmurs in the hallway,

"Oh yeah ... Lawline. That is the cheap, low-quality CLE provider." I guarantee those who said that had never seen one of our courses.

Now, we have won numerous awards and acclaim for technology, content, and our company culture and customer service. In 2018 and 2019, we were voted into the top three of online CLE providers in the country by the *National Law Journal*. At the same conferences where competitors once whispered disparagingly about us, we have been in leadership positions for years and are respected and admired by our peers.

Still, over a long period of time, instead of being energized by all that was going well, I was often down on myself for not being a better leader or doing enough for the business. In fact, when I read through my journals from 2006 to 2014, I did not recognize the person in much of the writing. I felt fear and often had a lack of focus as I faced each new challenge. *Sound familiar?*

From the surface, no one could tell this was going on. I remember one particular week when I had three friends tell me they wished they were in my shoes.

I went for a long walk with one of them. Noah told me that he felt like a failure. His wife felt that way about him too. He was not happy in his job. He was not happy with where he was at that point in his life.

At the time, I was being coached by Kim Ades of Frame of Mind Coaching™, who taught me the principles of thought management (see Chapter 2). I used everything I learned with her to try to change Noah's perception of his life. Not only did it not work, I felt like I was talking down to him because I was not as skilled as Kim.

Next, I tried another idea: sharing the not-so-glamorous side of running my business. I told him I lived with constant self-doubt in my leadership abilities. That led to anxiety, fear of failure, and the list went on.

When I shared with Noah that I was struggling with many thoughts and feelings similar to his, I saw it connect right away. All of a sudden, he was not alone in his feelings. I hope he felt he was in good company. From that moment on, we were able to work together to build his confidence and get him back to a place of self-worth. Doing that helped me as well, and now I hope it will help you.

The Benefit of Experience

I know today that I developed new leadership and entrepreneurial skills with each new experience and wall that I hit during that 11-year period with Lawline. All of those experiences pushed me forward. In 2014, we hired Mark Green, founder of Performance Dynamics Group, to coach our newly formed executive team, and that was the tipping point. Mark provided the missing component that helped transform me as a leader and led to significant business growth as a result.

Now, I want to reveal my stories to you. This practice was ingrained in me when I joined Entrepreneurs' Organization (EO) in 2008. (As I write this, I am the 2018–2019 president of the New York chapter.) The core tenet of EO is to not give advice, but to share experience. That helped inspire this book. In the pages that follow, I want to show you my own challenges, particularly those points when my stress and anxiety were high, and take you through my entire journey as an entrepreneur including the ups, the downs, and all of the lessons I learned, culminating in the FFwd Mindset!

Learning the Three Steps of the FFwd Mindset

The FFwd Mindset is built on the simple concept that we all want to fast-forward (FFwd) the impact we have on our business and the world around us. But those FFs have a bigger meaning: FEARLESS and FOCUS, the keys to taking control of your entrepreneurial impact. Ninety percent of the time, we are confident and feel we can take on the world. But this book is not about that 90 percent. Instead, it focuses on the 10 percent of the time when our fear and lack of focus prevent us from reaching our full potential in entrepreneurship and life. This leaves us stuck in our comfort zone, unable to push ahead to have the impact we have always dreamed about.

You can become fearless and focused by advancing through the three steps embodied in the FFwd Mindset. Step 1 is building your confidence so you can take action and get out of your comfort zone time and time again. In Step 2, you'll learn a surefire strategy for how to NIP Fear in the Bud when things get uncomfortable. In Step 3, you'll Find Your Focus, as I learned how to when I completed my first few marathons and later applied to Lawline in 2016 after we hired Mark.

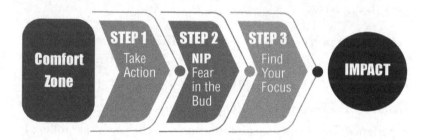

Become More Fearless and Focused Today

When I shifted my thinking from how do I get out of my comfort zone "for my own good," to how do I get out of my comfort zone "for the larger good," everything changed for me. The three steps of the Fast Forward mindset enhanced my personal and entrepreneurial impact immediately, and it will do the same for you.

STEP

1

TAKE ACTION

- No Labels
- Own Thoughts
- Makes You Special
- Take Action Now!

T aking action is what separates those who choose to stay in their comfort zones from those who break out of them. While it is simple to understand, the concept is anything but easy to actually live. In Step 1, I share with you four ways to build confidence in yourself so you will take action, not only now, but over and over again.

1 NO LABELS
(GOOD THING, BAD THING, WHO KNOWS?)

 15 *Minutes*

"Good thing, bad thing, who knows?"

I learned about this question in 2014 when I was attending an Entrepreneurs' Organization (EO) meeting at Nat Milner's restaurant, Gabriela's, on the Upper West Side of Manhattan. At EO's monthly events, we enjoy hearing talks from well-known or impactful people. On this occasion, Dr. Srikumar Rao, whose Creativity and Personal Mastery course is taught in many business schools, spoke to us about how to be happier in business and life.

As he sat onstage, Dr. Rao talked about that voice inside our heads— the one that is always there, always talking to you. He told us flat-out that we should not even try to subdue it. However, he went on to say there *is* something important that we can and *must* control to be happier and successful.

He shared an old parable about a Chinese farmer that went like this:

The Chinese farmer bought a horse from his neighbor, and the next day it escaped from the farm. The neighbor came over and said, "I am so sorry that happened! This is terrible!"

The farmer looked at him and said, "Good thing, bad thing, who knows?"

The next day the horse came back and brought several wild horses with it. The neighbor said, "Congratulations! That is amazing!"

Again, the farmer responded, "Good thing, bad thing, who knows?"

The farmer's son then rode one of the wild horses and promptly fell off and broke his arm. The neighbor said to the farmer, "I'm so sorry. That's horrible!"

The farmer again responded, "Good thing, bad thing, who knows?"

Finally, there was a war, and the neighbor's son was conscripted into the army. He ran over to the farmer and said, "You are so lucky! Your son doesn't have to go because he was injured!"

The farmer said again, "Good thing, bad thing, who knows?"

When you are open to not judging each situation or event as "good" or "bad," it allows you to take more action and gain as much experience as possible.

Dr. Rao explained the parable to us. "Whenever something happens in our life, we tend to put a label on it—a good thing or a bad thing. We label something bad up to 20 times more than we label it good." He went on. "Unfortunately, when we label something a bad thing, we experience it as a bad thing. The thing is, it might have not been bad if we did not label it as so in the first place."

When you are open to not judging each situation or event as "good" or "bad," it allows you to be more open to fearlessness and to gain as much experience as possible. *It gives you the confidence to keep moving forward out of your comfort zone.*

If you follow this philosophy, you are able to take the long view when things happen. You can say to yourself, "Just because it did not turn out the way I expected today, it does not mean it was bad. It might be the best thing that ever happened to me."

Doing this takes a lot of practice, patience, and understanding. It is about the long game. In the same way you do not become a basketball star or a pilot overnight, growing as an entrepreneur is a lifelong journey. The good news is this technique is something that you can start today. I know because when I adopted this mindset, I started taking more action on things outside my comfort zone.

From Pride to Despair and Back: My First "Good Thing, Bad Thing" Experience

My "good thing, bad thing, who knows?" story starts in 2003 when I was attending New York Law School. After working in sales for five years after graduating college, I was not satisfied. I also noticed that a lot of my friends were not happy in their jobs, either, with no way out. I decided to go to law school because I saw it as my best opportunity for building a long-term career to support my family. I not only would focus on studying the law, but would throw myself into going "above and beyond" where I could.

A big opportunity for doing that presented itself during my second year. Moot Court is a student club where you compete with other schools arguing each side of a trial with mock judges. Unafraid of public speaking, I knew I would quickly excel in this arena. Full of passion and a sense of mission, I studied the trial briefs day and night as I practiced for the qualifying competition. When the big day came, I was brimming with confidence and felt myself doing very well in each round.

I walked out of there feeling great.

A few days before the organizers were to announce the winners, one of the student leaders met with me privately where she said, "Congratulations, David! You scored enough points and have made it! I would like to invite you and your family to the awards ceremony where we announce all the winners who are the next members of the team."

I cannot tell you how proud I was after hearing that. I now had a clear path for the next two years of school—one that would not only allow me to meet so many more students, but also would lead me to the impact I had envisioned when I applied for law school.

The following week, I brought my wife to the awards ceremony before an enthusiastic audience of about 300 people. The room was packed, and I was psyched. As the hosts started calling all of the winners to stage, my wife grabbed my hand, smiled, and kissed me on the cheek. She was beaming with pride. When the ceremony ended, everyone applauded and all of the students left the stage.

There was only one major problem: *they never called my name!*

Assuming it was just a mistake, I made my way through a crowd to the team's student organizer standing near the front of the room. When I let her know about the error, her eyes widened and her face went completely white. "Oh my God, you are right! There has been an error." She hesitated for a second, and blurted, "You actually did not make the team as there was a problem with how they scored it. You were supposed to be notified yesterday about what happened. I am so sorry that you had to come today."

WAIT ... WHAT???!

I was in shock. But, I still felt confident. My wife was next to me, and heck, I was already here and this was a student organization. I had no doubt they would make an exception for me, especially considering what had just gone down. I started explaining all of this to the organizer, who looked at me politely, saying nothing at first. A few other organizers walked over and joined us, but after 15 minutes of pleading my case, they would not budge. I did not make the team. I walked out with my head down, humiliated and defeated.

As I walked down the streets of downtown Manhattan, all the emotions hit me and I started crying. The network that I had envisioned for the next two-plus years was gone.

I was devastated at that moment. However, it ultimately motivated me to take matters into my own hands and build my own network when that opportunity presented itself. Although I didn't describe it as such then, it was the first "good thing, bad thing, who knows?" experience that led to my entrepreneur path today.

Getting Thrown Out of My Internship: A Bad Thing, or...?

In my second summer of law school, I got a job at a law firm specializing in real estate. My job there was to represent banks during property transactions. When you buy a property in New York City, the paperwork is enormous. It's a lot to keep track of, and it all must be signed and put in the proper order. At first, this actually seemed like a great experience. They sent me on my own to closings even though I was still a law student. However, I learned quickly that it was not for me. I am what you call a "big picture guy," and making sure all the t's were crossed and i's were dotted was not in my wheelhouse.

So, I decided to give notice that I would leave the internship at the end of the summer.

Early one morning, I entered the building with the intent of communicating my decision to my supervising attorney, a large, imposing guy in a dark suit and power tie. I walked into his office and asked to talk. He gave me kind of a funny look and told me to close the door. I faced him and sputtered out the big news. "Michael, I have decided to put all my energy into my classes for my third year and I will not be able to stay at this internship through the school year."

There was a short, uncomfortable pause as his eyes narrowed. Then, "YOU ARE NOT STAYING ON????!" he screamed so loudly that everyone in the office had to have heard. In fact, I thought I could hear the buzz of office conversations outside the door come to a terrifying halt. "THE ONLY REASON I HIRED YOU THIS SUMMER WAS TO STAY DURING THE YEAR!!!" he bellowed, his face red with indignation.

The screaming seemed to go on for hours, but in reality was probably only a few minutes. Although there were still a couple of weeks left to the summer, he told me to leave the office that minute. Stunned, I opened his door, and ventured out into the office area, keeping my head down in order to avoid the stares of my coworkers. I did not say a word to the many people I had worked with all summer as I made my way to the refuge of the elevator. I silently took it down to the lobby and headed, brutally alone, into the streets of Manhattan.

A bad thing, for sure ... or was it?

Over the next couple of days, I thought about what had happened and gradually came to what turned out to be a life-changing realization: As much as I could help it, I was NEVER going to put myself in that situation again. I wanted to control my work environment and do something I was passionate about and proud of. I also realized that becoming a partner at many law firms was similar to being a salesperson—you still had to identify and pitch potential clients in addition to all of the legal work!

This revelation rekindled my childhood dream of starting my own business and becoming an entrepreneur. So this "bad thing" actually turned out to be good, and it is still paying off!

At the time, however, I did not know where or how to start on my new dream. And, I was going into my third year of law school, so I had no spare time. That meant that the chances of starting my own business while avoiding working for an attorney were close to zero. Or so I thought.

The First "Bad Thing" Payoff: TrueNYC and a New Path

Over the years, I have read a lot of self-help and business books. During law school, several of those inspired me, *but* they did not tell me how to start a business. One such book was *Rich Dad Poor Dad* by Robert Kiyosaki. *I loved that book.* It showed me the importance of having your money work for you while not working for someone else. It was exactly the mindset I wanted at that point in my life. However, Kiyosaki would write something like "I started business X ... *yada, yada, yada* ... and I was soon making money hand over fist." The part that I really wanted to learn about was the mechanics of actually making business successful, and his *yada, yada, yada* was, unfortunately, way more general. The more I looked into other books that I had read, the more I realized that the truly substantive information was missing there too. So who was going to fill that void, and how?

When I was a kid back in the pre-internet days of 1980s cable television, my dad, Alan Schnurman, had a local public access TV show called *Lawline*, where he would discuss current events and legal topics with prominent judges and attorneys. It built his reputation and stature in the legal field, as everyone wanted to be on his show. I've got to give him credit: He was *way* ahead of his time and was spending thousands of dollars a month keeping the project

rience. I focus on that quite a bit in the coming pages. To read about the five themes of success I learned during these interviews visit ffwdmindset.com/resources.

The Crash and Rebirth of Lawline

My next big "good thing, bad thing, who knows?" experience proved to me that even when things seem to fall apart, you're never really out of the game.

In 1999 my mom, along with dad and his law firm partner, Ben, decided to place a big bet during the first round of the dot-com bubble. Tech companies were forming fast, going public, and building a lot of traction. It was the same year Mark Cuban sold Broadcast.com to Yahoo! for $5.7 billion. It was also the same year that continuing legal education became mandatory in New York State. My dad was a frequent lecturer at bar associations and recognized it as a huge opportunity. With the sale of Broadcast.com and other online-streaming platforms, he recognized that the future of education would be on the internet. It was at that point he decided to bring his TV show online as a CLE provider in New York and sell courses to attorneys. Of course, it was a great idea. My dad was once again ahead of his time.

However, after the bubble burst in 2000, the dream of going public, making millions of dollars, and retiring, vanished. But it was even worse than that: things were falling apart at the business. It was bringing in a couple of thousand dollars per month, but server costs and software licenses were so expensive that Lawline was losing money each year. Still, my dad didn't want to shut it down even though that's exactly what everyone wanted him to do. He knew he had something special and did not want to throw it away.

My dad and his partners ultimately dissolved the corporation and went back to practicing law, while my mom continued to produce the

Lawline TV show, maintaining a dozen courses that were still being sold on the website at a loss.

This was a bad thing, right? We all thought so at the time.

Then, in 2006, while doing my entrepreneur interviews during my last year of law school, an idea took shape. *I could take the same cheap camera, but this time interview attorneys and turn the footage into online CLE courses.* Although it did not work for my dad, I figured with my past internet experience and the availability of cheaper technology, I could succeed with it. Since CLE is mandatory in New York, I would have a market of 130,000 attorneys. I remember thinking if Lawline can make a few thousand dollars a month with nobody really focusing on it, imagine what it can do if I put even half my energy into making it a success.

The first challenge was deciding how to move forward. I could do it 100 percent on my own, call it TrueCLE, and have full ownership, or I could take the existing Lawline brand, which they had grown, and blow it through the roof. To me it was a no-brainer to build on the established brand, so we came up with a fair arrangement, I created a new company, and I hit the ground running.

I changed servers and built a new website on the cheap. By the time I graduated from law school in May of 2006, I had everything I needed to feel confident in giving this new, exciting venture a go. My plan was in place.

School ended. I studied my ass off for three months, then took and passed the bar. Starting that fall, I put everything I had into making Lawline a success.

In California's Silicon Valley, you start a business in a garage. In the world of New York's Silicon Alley, you do it in a kitchen! Since I was just getting started, we needed to keep our costs low, so I convinced my dad to let me take over the kitchen in his office. One weekend, I moved in and set up a couple of desks. I remember being on the phones with customers while lawyers were coming in and washing their dishes. It was quite a scene!

Only a few months into the new business, I had one of those moments where you pinch yourself. After that legal internship debacle, I decided to become an entrepreneur, taking control of my life to have more personal freedom. I took action by starting an entrepreneur TV show to get the answers, and here I was at the next stage, making it happen!

I knew things were going to move quickly when, after only 90 days in the business, we were bringing in $10,000/month. I took my wife out to one of the most expensive restaurants in the city to celebrate, and I remember thinking "it cannot get much better than this."

Of course, we were only getting started!

The Bad Things Made Me President of EO

Thanks to my interviews with scores of entrepreneurs for TrueNYC, I built a network of amazing people. That is how I met Len Oppenheimer, who was manning a booth for EO at a Crain's Business conference. I told him about my interviews, and he invited me to the next board meeting to share what I was doing. Before I knew it, I was interviewing almost a dozen entrepreneurs from EO. Each person was more interesting than the next, and I knew this was an organization I would join one day if I ever had the opportunity.

One entrepreneur I had interviewed for TrueNYC was Matthew J. Weiss who had a law firm, 888-Red-Light, which fought traffic tickets. As a law student, I was taken in by his story of not going the traditional highbrow route as a lawyer and becoming even more successful than most of his peers. We bonded right away.

As it happens, two years later he became president of the EO New York chapter and called to let me know about its newly formed accelerator program. It did not require the typical $1 million in revenue to become a member, but instead would bring you in with only $250,000.

Lawline had just surpassed $250,000 in revenue, so I said "yes" without hesitation. I was fortunate to become a full-fledged EONY member the very next year since the business was growing like crazy. After five years of membership, I was asked to join the board. Four years later, I was elected president of the chapter and started my official role on July 1, 2018.

One thing leads to another ... and another. I was rejected from Moot Court. I was thrown out of a lawyer's office. The original incarnation of Lawline didn't succeed financially. In the moment, these experiences could have been labeled "bad," but they led me to the path of entrepreneurship and the EONY presidency by the time I was 40.

In hindsight, these "bad things" were the best things that ever could have happened to me.

What are things in your life that have been labeled bad? What are you hesitating to take action on because you are "afraid" of a bad result? Remove these labels and you are well on your way to taking more action to fast-forward your impact on the world around you.

▶**ACTION STEP:** Start using *Good Thing, Bad Thing, Who Knows?* in your daily vocabulary.

---

2 TAKE OWNERSHIP OF YOUR THOUGHTS

 *8 Minutes*

1. Connect Your Thoughts to Outcomes
2. Learn How to Deal with Things Out of Your Control
3. Make Bold Decisions
4. Visualize Your Future Success

The world's most successful people understand that when you *own your thoughts*, you are able to unlock the power of your mind to create the very outcomes you visualize. In this chapter, I take you through four mental strategies to make that happen.

Thoughts ▸ Beliefs ▸ Actions ▸ Outcomes

1. Connect Your Thoughts to Outcomes

When I first started working with Kim Ades, she helped me learn a simple but fundamental concept: Our thoughts lead to our beliefs, which lead to our actions, which lead to our outcomes. This means that all outcomes begin with our *thoughts*. That makes our thoughts very powerful.

Owning your thinking and reducing negative self-talk will be a life-long journey for you. (It is for all of us.) The key thing to remember is that when you are not where you want to be—for example, when your inner voice tells you "my business isn't growing fast enough," or "I don't know how to fire my #2"—do not focus first on simply changing the outcomes you've been dealt. Instead, *examine the thinking that led you to those outcomes.*

Maybe you are not growing fast enough because you are afraid to take bigger risks than you already have, or you have not fired your #2 because you do not believe you have the leadership skills to run your company on your own or even find a suitable replacement. For every outcome challenge, you need to identify what thinking has led to it.

Do not focus on changing the outcomes you've been dealt. Examine the thinking that led to those outcomes.

This approach is reinforced in Jack Canfield's best-selling book, *The Success Principles: How to Get from Where You Are to Where You Want to Be.* In fact, Principle 1 is "Take 100 percent ownership for your life." Jack points out that too often in life we do not take ownership for exactly where we are at any given time and instead find someone or something else to blame.

▶**EXERCISE:** Connecting Your Thoughts to Outcomes

Here is a simple exercise to help you identify how your thinking can lead to your desired outcomes.

1. Take a blank piece of paper and put a line down the center. At the top of the page, label the left column "Thoughts and Beliefs." Label the right column "Actions and Outcomes."

2. In the right column, list all of the actions you want to take or outcomes you want to achieve in your life. (Do not overthink this as it should just be a brain dump.)

3. To the left of each outcome, write the number one thought, assumption, or belief that could prevent you from getting there.

Keep this piece of paper as we will come back to it later. To download a template for this, visit ffwdmindset.com/resources.

Thoughts and Beliefs #1 Fear	Actions and Outcomes
Crashing Very little sales	Becoming a Pilot Publishing a Book

2. Learn How to Deal with Things Out of Your Control

I'm sure you would love for your business to progress in a straight line upward all the time, but the course of true success is more like climbing a mountain—generally up but with ridges, walls, and valleys along the way.

Many times these walls and valleys are the situations that you do not control, and they often get in your way even if you have fully planned something to a "T." For example, they could be when an employee exits the company without warning, leaving you in the lurch, or when a weak economy leads to lower sales. They can arise from unexpected regulatory hurdles. These are the standard "ins and outs" of everyday business that you cannot control.

To help deal with events outside your control, Jack offers the formula E+R=O (Event + Response = Outcome). For example, if you are stuck in traffic and you are late for a meeting, you can respond by screaming and honking your horn, and as a result your outcome is to feel angry and upset. Or, you can decide to accept that you can't control traffic and respond by being productive and listening to an audiobook. With the latter choice, the outcome is that you will enjoy a restful calm and learn something new.

Jack explains that you can't control the weather, the stock market, or politics. You cannot control your spouse, parents, boss, or employees. But as I learned from him and Kim, the three things you can control are your thoughts, beliefs, and (re)actions. When you control these, you control the outcomes.

The same principles work for companies as well as individuals. Jim Collins, in his book, *Great by Choice*, wanted to see if companies that are more successful than others have more good luck than those that aren't. After doing all their research, what they found is that all companies have about the same amount of good luck and bad luck. However, *how the companies handled and responded to the bad luck* made all the difference regarding who was most successful. He called this Return on Luck (ROL).

3. Make Bold Decisions

After I fired my first COO, I remember sitting down with my dad during lunch at a nice Chinese restaurant near my office—a place where we met regularly to discuss business. We now had a 20-person sales team that needed to be managed.

I was trying to update their sales compensation plan and I was stuck. I couldn't decide what to do, and as a result, my indecision caused a lot of stress because I kept thinking about it. I also didn't give a clear message to the team, and it was causing me to back up on other important decisions. It was the equivalent of having clogged pipes.

"In 50 years, the decisions you make today are not going to mean anything."

One of the pieces of advice my dad gave me during that time was simply, "You have to make a decision because if you don't decide, then nothing is going to happen and you're not going to be able to move forward."

He added, "In 50 years, whatever decisions you make today are not going to mean anything. They're not going to matter."

This attitude toward decision-making is a key component of taking action to break out of your comfort zone. It's all about recognizing how each mistake or wrong turn is not going to wreck your life. Rather, these decisions are about learning and should be embraced. You're going to learn from them either way.

One book that embraces the philosophy well is Dale Carnegie's, *How to Stop Worrying and Start Living*. He breaks down two formulas that have allowed me to get out of my comfort zone time and time again. The first formula is how to make decisions and act upon them. The second is a technique that can be used to reduce your worry about the consequences of a wrong decision.

Formula 1: Make Bold Decisions

1. First and foremost, get the facts. Carnegie noted that "half the worry in the world is caused by people trying to make decisions before they have sufficient knowledge on which to base them."

2. Once you have carefully weighed all of the facts, make your decision.

3. Once you have carefully made your decision, you must act! At that point you need to forge ahead and ignore any anxiety you may have about the outcome.

Formula 2: Worry Less about the Consequences of a Wrong Decision

1. Ask yourself, "What is the worst that can possibly happen if I can't solve my problem?"

2. Prepare yourself mentally to accept the worst, if necessary.

3. Then calmly try to improve upon the worst, which you have already mentally agreed to accept.

Try using either of these formulas the next time you are stuck making a decision. It will free you up to take the action required to get out of your comfort zone.

4. Visualize Your Future Success

The first thing Kim made me do when we started working together was an exercise where I had to pretend it was five years in the future, and I was to tell the story of my accomplishments as if they had already occurred. When you think of your goals in that way, there are no walls in your head to prevent you from accomplishing them. It was one of the most freeing things I have ever done.

The book *The Secret* repeats this concept, as does Napoleon Hill's classic, *Think and Grow Rich*, which was written 70 years before it. The concept is simple. In order for something to happen, you have to believe in your mind and *act like it already has happened*. Then, the universe will move out of its way to manifest your belief into reality.

You need to believe that you are going to grow a $100 million company! You do that by envisioning that you already have done it. *You need to believe* you are going to buy the house of your dreams by envisioning that you already have it. And, of course, the list goes on and on.

I am already anticipating the skeptics pushing back at this as "wishful thinking" without any real-world merit. And I get that, which is why I want to direct you to Gina Mollicone-Long's book *Think or Sink*, which uses science to support the concept. Mollicone-Long shares that you can only absorb 126 bits per second of information out of literally millions of bits surrounding you in any moment. There are two great examples that bring this concept to life, and I will share them with you by actually having you do them both.

▶**EXERCISE:** Focusing Your Perception

Look around the room and find everything that is blue. Give yourself 30 seconds and memorize everything, but do not write it down. While you're doing that, put this book down. After you have taken the 30 seconds to memorize everything that was blue, and only then, turn the page.

Now, without looking around the room, write below everything that you saw that was yellow.

List

_____

_____

_____

_____

_____

_____

I predict that you may able to remember a few of the yellow things, but certainly not all of them.

This is the point: When you are focusing on what is blue, you do not pay attention to what is yellow. In the same way, if you are only focusing on how your company is *not* growing fast enough, you are not going to be able to focus on all the opportunities for growth all around you.

▶**EXERCISE:** Seeing What's Right in Front of You

There is a famous thirty-second video popularized by Christopher Chabris and Daniel Simons in their 2010 book, *The Invisible Gorilla*, of kids passing around a basketball. Go to ffwdmindset.com/resources now and watch it. DO IT NOW. GET ON YOUR PHONE (I know it is next to you) AND WATCH. Do not read any further. CLOSE THE BOOK until you've watched the video!

Did you see it? Maybe you did, maybe you did not. This experiment found that only about 50 percent of people actually see the gorilla walking across the basketball court as the players are passing the ball. Don't believe me? Watch it again. The lesson is similar to the last lesson in that when you are focused on the ball being passed, sometimes you miss what is right in front of you. (By the way, Chabris and Simons won a Nobel Prize for this experiment!)

I have had this book written in my head since I was in college. In my vision, the book sold over a million copies, and it was the first of many. In my vision of the future, I toured the world and impacted millions of people with the book and my teachings. In my own mind, *it already happened*, and now I am just playing out the movie that has been in my head my whole life. You get what I am saying? If you want to take action to break through your comfort zone, you need to believe that it has already happened.

In Chapter 1, you learned the importance of not labeling any situation as bad. In this chapter, you learned how to own your thoughts to build your confidence. In Chapter 3, I dive into understanding what makes you special and how to use that to your advantage.

3 KNOW WHAT MAKES YOU SPECIAL

 *12 Minutes*

answered my phone after the fourth ring. "Hey David, it's Jonathan. I wanted to see if I could stop by your office and talk over how things are going on the sales team." Right away red flags went up. I had made it clear to our entire 40-person company that if anybody wanted to talk, my door was always open. This was especially important because our sales team was a few blocks away in a different office, and I only ended up seeing them a few times a week. With that said, this was the first time a salesperson had reached out to me to discuss how things were going.

"Sure, no problem, Jonathan," I said, and we set a time to talk the next day.

A few hours later, I spoke with our COO, William, who was in charge of the sales team and mentioned Jonathan's call. I did not realize until later, but THAT WAS A MISTAKE. If Jonathan had called me directly, there was a reason he did not want William involved.

I first met William when looking for an apartment and he was a top real estate broker. As he took me from one property to another, I remember thinking "this guy sounds like an owner." He was great at selling without "selling," if you know what I mean. He had a light touch, clearly cared about what he was talking about, and was very likable right away.

I let him know we were starting to build a sales team at Lawline and asked if he could get involved. He responded that he could consult with us part-time and would be happy to train our staff. That part-time gig turned into a full-time VP of sales role, and before long, we had a 20-person sales team in a different office generating $1 million a year in revenue. When I realized that William was doing much more than sales, I quickly promoted him to COO to help not just with the growth of the sales team, but with the company as a whole.

Now, on this particular day, before I knew it, William had convinced me to *not* meet with Jonathan, stating that he would work with him to help resolve the issue. As William put it, "You are the CEO, and you need to keep focused on the big picture, not the day-to-day challenges of the sales team." So, I let Jonathan know that he should talk to William, and if there were still any issues I would be happy to jump in.

Commitment broken!

I had just broken the commitment to my open-door policy. I thought I was being a good leader by delegating. I listened to my COO. I doubted my own decisions, and as a result, I allowed William to change my mind. Again, this was another red flag I did not see at the time.

A couple of weeks went by, and at a company culture event, another member of the sales team told Olivia, our customer service manager, that some colleagues were stealing leads from our marketing campaigns and claiming them as their own.

Wait. *What?*

After two days of investigation, it became clear that something was not right. We dug further and discovered a loophole in the system that was allowing a number of salespeople to claim marketing leads as their own. Worse, almost everyone on the team knew this had been going on for a long period of time. Not surprisingly, the three salespeople involved had been our "top performers." They were all fired immediately.

As the day came to an end, my head was spinning. How did we get to this point? How did I let my sales culture get so infected? Yes, they were in a different office, but that was no excuse. The problems always start at the top.

I had allowed this to happen even though I observed multiple red flags indicating that William was not running the office in a professional or productive manner. In my head, I had ignored the warning signs, continuing to tell myself that "this is sales culture, and it is just different."

In fact, I had observed that the sales revenue kept "increasing" and decided that I would let William do his thing while I did mine. The truth was I did not have the mental tools or the focus to know how to have regular one-on-one meetings with William. And without that, he ran his sales office as he saw fit. When I look back on this now, I realize that I did not have the confidence to trust my own instincts—to act on the things I saw right before my eyes! Instead, I deferred to William, who I saw as the "expert" in his area.

While there were a few bad apples, most of the sales team was made up of good people. In all honesty, it was a positive sign that members of the team disclosed what the others were doing when they had seen enough of the cheating. Things had to change, and they had to change quickly!

On Saturday morning, I woke up early and realized there was no easy way out of this situation. William had to go, and he had to go before Monday. William claimed he knew nothing about the scheme, but I didn't buy that, as he was very smart. But regardless if he knew or if he did not know, it truly did not matter to me. The real challenge was that the culture in the office had to change right away. I had believed in William, so this was certainly a low moment for me in my young company's history.

On Monday morning, I called the entire sales team to the main office and explained the situation. "Fred, Lisa, and Matthew were let go on Friday. This weekend, I told William not to come back either. What happened within the sales team was unacceptable. I apologize for letting it get that far. Today, we turn over a new leaf. Today will be the first day of a new culture and a new energy for the sales team. I will be working with the team on a regular basis as we rebuild our culture and trust."

I committed to working with the team and helping it get back on track. I did my best. I showed up there almost every day for the next few months and invested in each team member. The challenge was that I was not a sales manager, and the dramatic experience the team had gone through made it hard to recover. Half of the team resigned within six months.

I was not proud of how it ended with William or the sales team. It was quite painful and it still is when I look back on how I handled some of those situations. The thing is, William understood how to get people to do what he wanted, while at the same time giving tough love when needed. He knew how to energize and motivate. He was a great salesperson. These were skills I felt that I lacked.

However, instead of recognizing that similar to me, William had strengths and weaknesses, I created a superhero picture of him in my mind. "If he is stronger than I am in this, then he must be stronger than I am in everything. He can do no wrong. He is a superhero." This mindset prevented me from taking action with William and the sales team until it was too late.

Of course, this was not the only time I felt like a "failure" in business. It was not until a candid conversation with my dad years later that it hit me how common this feeling was, and my dad shared with me the ultimate reason why I felt this way. Once again, an exercise I did with Kim Ades helped me build confidence by recognizing what makes me special, and it can do the same for you.

You Don't Know How Good You Are!

One sunny afternoon several years ago, I was sitting on my back deck with my father, and I was in one of my low moments—the 10 percent you don't often read about in success books. I decided to confide in him. "Dad, I am frustrated with being so hard on myself each day. To be honest, I feel like a failure more than a winner."

This was not just about what happened in the past. Each and every day I was finding things that I could have done better. These normally stemmed from breaking commitments to myself or from knowing I was not living up to my potential.

There is no winning and there is no losing. There is just gaining more experience!

As I kept sharing with my dad, I did have a glimmer of hope. I had been reading through my old journals and identifying all of the walls I had faced that I could not break through. And then it hit me. "This is all part of the process," I told him. "Every wall that I faced and could not break through is not a failure. It is just an opportunity to gain more experience." Again, "Good thing, bad thing, who knows?"

My dad listened like a village elder. He rubbed his chin, rocked in his chair, looked at me, and intoned, "Go on."

I declared, "At the end of the day, there is no winning and there is no losing. There is just gaining more experience!"

"Exactly," my dad responded. "My experience has proven that if you try ten things, four are pushes, two are losses, two are singles or doubles, but one or two are home runs." I had heard him say this one before and I liked the simplicity of the analogy. He continued, "The thing is, you never know which one is going to be the home run, so you have to keep trying new things."

Now I was listening intently because he certainly knew of what he spoke. He came from no money, paid for his law school by driving a taxi, then started his own law firm almost right after passing the bar. When he was younger, he read up on the Forbes 100 richest people, and he noticed that many of them were involved in real estate. So he got out of his own comfort zone to follow that path. He invested in real estate whenever he had extra money from his practice. Over the years, this side project got bigger and bigger, until at one point he was the largest owner of developable land in the Hamptons area called Sagaponack. In 2018, this area was identified by the real estate website, Property Shark, as one of the most expensive residential zip codes in the country.

So I offered an important follow-up question. "Dad, you have done huge real estate deals that most people would not have the risk tolerance to handle. How did you know you could handle it?"

He looked at me and had a moment of honesty as well. "Every day, I have to reprogram myself to be fearless because inside, I am a scared little boy." He explained that he repeats these quotes when he feels that fear:

Your attitude equals your altitude.

I can. I will. I must.

Optimism is the faith that leads to achievement. Nothing can be done without hope and confidence. — Helen Keller

"However, Dave, there is something else you are missing, and it is the most important part," he continued. "Listen closely because I have told you this several times before." With that, my dad said seven words the led me on my current journey to FFwd my impact. "Dave, you don't know how good you are!"

"You don't know how good you are!"

As he was saying it, he could see me pushing back. I do not like to be complimented as it generally makes me uncomfortable. "I know, I know," I said rather dismissively. My dad could tell I was trying to deflect as I normally do.

He pushed harder. "Dave, I mean it. You do stuff I could never do. Look what you have built with Lawline. Look at the entrepreneurs you have surrounded yourself with, your amazing family. Heck, we are sitting in the home you dreamed about since you were a kid."

He continued his impassioned plea. "Instead of spending all your time thinking about what you are not doing right, focus on what *is* going right in your life. That starts with recognizing how good you are."

The Imposter Syndrome

As my dad kept talking, the wheels started spinning in my head. That phrase, "You don't know how good you are," sounded very familiar, and I was trying to figure out when I heard it last. Then it hit me. I was sitting in my bedroom with my wife and she was crying.

Not about the kids or the family, but about a presentation she had to do at work.

I knew Kelli had a fear of public speaking, so I was used to that, but this time I could sense that her anxiety was greater than usual. She was doing a presentation at her hospital to the board of advisors based on something positive her department had recently done. But because of the audience, the pressure was significantly higher than in her regular meetings.

I knew her problem wasn't focus because she had the presentation memorized. So I looked at her and said, "Kel, what are you afraid of?"

She looked at me, took a long pause, and said, "I am afraid when I talk I will sound inarticulate. And when that happens, they are going to realize I am a fraud and I have been one for the past fourteen years."

WHAT??? I heard my wife say that and I got chills. Kelli is one of the smartest people I know. She has been promoted numerous times, once won social worker of the year, was handpicked for this position, and regularly gets accolades from her colleagues.

I stared directly into Kelli's eyes and said, "Kel, you don't know how good you are." After the conversation, I called Kim and she worked with Kelli for three days to help her build confidence in herself and to identify what makes her special. The main technique she used with her over and over again was Dale Carnegie's formula to reduce worry, which I share at the end of Chapter 2. It worked! Kelli went into that presentation calmer and more confident than for any presentation in her past few years in that role.

As I was sitting there with my dad on the deck, it hit me like a ton of bricks. It is not just Kelli, and it is not just me. ALL of us do not realize how good we are. In fact, according to the *Journal of Behav-*

ioral Science, 70 percent of the general population has experienced *imposter syndrome:* that feeling that you aren't worthy or are even a fraud. It is one of the most common walls that people and entrepreneurs face. Looking back to when I first started working with Kim, there was an exercise that dealt with this mental challenge head-on.

▶**EXERCISE:** What Makes Me Special?

The confidence-building exercise with Kim involved asking those closest to me what makes me special. She had me email three family members, three people I have known for a long time, and three people with whom I have worked, asking them all what they think I am good at.

Below is the paragraph I sent to them.

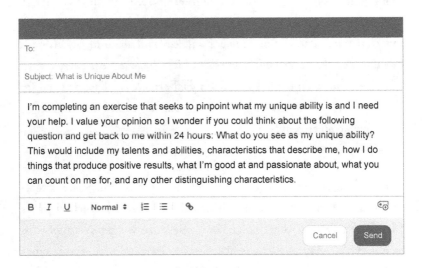

To:

Subject: What is Unique About Me

I'm completing an exercise that seeks to pinpoint what my unique ability is and I need your help. I value your opinion so I wonder if you could think about the following question and get back to me within 24 hours: What do you see as my unique ability? This would include my talents and abilities, characteristics that describe me, how I do things that produce positive results, what I'm good at and passionate about, what you can count on me for, and any other distinguishing characteristics.

B *I* U   Normal ⇕   ≣ ≣ ❧

Cancel   Send

The responses I got felt great. People saw things in me that I did not see in myself or stated their comments in ways that were inspiring for me. Also, when people from all different walks of life said similar good things about me, it really hit home.

After my conversation with my dad years later, I took the time to turn all the emails into two paragraphs, put them all in first person, and refer to them on a regular basis. Here they are:

How I Am with Others

I surround myself with great people and I am passionate about making them better. I am a person magnet. I am a people person. I am kind and caring. I make people feel comfortable. People trust me and want to be around me. I inspire others. I allow others to see and enjoy life while pursuing a mission of value. I never make someone feel stupid. I am a great motivator. I am a loyal friend. I am fun to be around. It is easy for others to be themselves around me.

My Skills

I am a great communicator. I have a very positive "can do" attitude. I deal well with adversity. I deal well with pressure. I can laugh at myself. I am a learner. I am not afraid to know something. I try to understand things. If I am interested in a topic, I will learn all about it. My vision is learning and the never-ending pursuit of it. I have a great energy level. I have a great work-life balance. I am goal-oriented. I have passion for doing my best. I like creating. I am a great networker. I am great at interviewing other people.

Many of the statements generated by this exercise rang true. I realized that I already knew these things about myself, but many times I had been unable to verbalize them. Because we get so caught up in our day-to-day challenges, we need to be reminded about what makes us special on a regular basis. These serve as the perfect reminders. Reviewing this exercise helped reinforce that champion voice inside my head that knew I was capable of so much more and wanted to FFwd my impact.

Recognizing How Good You Are

Recognizing how good you are, and that you have unique traits that make you special, is one of the foundational concepts for building your self-confidence. The more confidence you have, the easier it will be to take action to get out of your comfort zone over and over again. One of the most important things you can take from this book is this exercise. I paid thousands of dollars to get this advice from an amazing coach, and I am giving it to you. Send the emails now! Download the email template at ffwdmindset.com/resources.

In the two previous chapters, you learned how to build confidence in yourself and your decisions by 1) not labeling a situation as bad, and 2) owning your thoughts. In Chapter 4, I share with you what you need to do to take action NOW to break out of your comfort zone.

4 TAKE ACTION NOW!

 *11 Minutes*

t was snowing sideways as my friend and I drove, very slowly, through a major nor'easter down I-95 from New York City to Washington, DC. It was white-knuckle time all the way, with huge trucks passing us on the left and right. Still, I was intent on seeing Jack Canfield speak at his One Day to Greatness event in the nation's capital because of the impact his book *The Success Principles* has had on my success and happiness.

We finally made it to Washington, and Jack didn't disappoint as he addressed an enthusiastic audience of 500 people. He touched on numerous important points throughout the day, but the one that resonated with me the most was what he shared with us first thing in the morning.

When he took the stage, he looked at the crowd and stated, "Most of you are not where you want to be because you are addicted to comfort. Most of you stay in your comfort zone."

Jack went on to show us how easy it is for something that at first feels *uncomfortable* to go away. He said, "I want everyone to interlock their hands together. Do it a few times." I did what he suggested a few times in a row and it was easy enough.

Jack continued. "When you do it, you will generally have the same thumb on top. Now I want you to do it again, but this time put the other thumb on top." He looked over the audience as we followed his instructions.

"Feels weird, right?" And yes it did. In fact, when I switched it from my right to my left thumb on top, it felt like it was someone else's. Jack continued, "Here is the interesting part. If you were to leave your hand with this opposite thumb on top for five minutes, that weird feeling would go away. It would just feel normal." I did it, and once again, he was right it. Don't believe me? Try it now!

He went on to say what I have already known for years, and what we all know deep inside: *You have to be willing to do the uncomfortable things that make you grow.*

That got me to thinking about another best-selling author and motivational speaker, Craig Valentine, who jumped out of his own comfort zone when he decided to quit his well-paying nine-to-five job to pursue his dream to be a national motivational speaker. Determined to get on his new path, he walked into his manager's office one day and told him that he was going to resign. Craig was a valuable employee, so his boss wasn't hearing it and offered him a nice salary increase. Craig thought for a few seconds, then politely declined. His boss came back with an even better offer. Again, Craig held his ground and declined. So, the boss tried again and again, the fourth offer was so much money that Craig hesitated.

He went home that night to discuss it with his wife. They both realized that the offer amounted to much more money than he would make in a long time (if ever) being a motivational speaker, and the "smart" thing to do would be to take it. However, he went in the next day, thanked his manager, but said he was going to pursue his dream.

At that moment, Craig realized something important and he shared it in one of his talks: "I was almost too good to be great. I was almost too comfortable in my good life to reach my greatness."

"I was almost too comfortable in my good life to reach my greatness."

In 1999, Craig went on to compete in Toastmasters' World Championship for Public Speaking against 25,000 other speakers, and as fate would have it, he won. As they say, the rest is history, and he became a world-renowned motivational speaker, just as he had dreamed.

WOW. Craig's story of saying those words and boldly taking action to pursue his greatness really inspired me when I first heard it. I hope you feel the same way reading about it now.

When it came to entrepreneurship, the biggest struggle I faced was leading others, as well as having enough confidence in myself to make the tougher decisions to grow my company. You can read about building a business, about becoming a great leader, about making hard decisions, but until you take action and experience it in the real world you are not going to grow.

The Lightning Bolt

When I was 20, I truly thought I would be making seven figures within a few years of graduating college. I did go from $27,000 to $65,000 during that period, which I was proud of, BUT it was a far cry from where I wanted to be.

As I mentioned previously, during the discussion with my dad on the back deck, something happened that led me to write this book. "Dad, my 20-year-old self would definitely be proud of what I've accomplished, but at this stage," I told him, " I expected to have a bigger business and have more impact on the communities I touch."

He pushed back right away, and rather directly. "Do you know how many people would want to achieve what you have achieved, and have what you have?" I thought about that for a while, and then it was as if a lightning bolt hit me. I realized I was expressing the same story I had about myself when I was 20, but now my expectations had increased 100 times. On the one hand, this is what makes entrepreneurs good at what they do—the fact that they always want to have more impact. On the other hand, it leads to a disconnect if the actions you take don't support the story of yourself you have in your head, and if your actions directly contradict that story.

My dad has been extremely successful in many areas, but I think that his biggest accomplishment in life has been his optimistic attitude—supporting his drive to get out of his comfort zone and take some risks. It is this attitude that is completely tied to the actions and outcomes he has experienced. It is because of his attitude and his entrepreneurial success that he has been such a strong mentor and influence since I started my journey 11 years ago.

What will be your "quit my job" moment?

I came to realize that my real issue was not that I wanted a bigger business or more notoriety—of course, positive only!—though I certainly wouldn't complain if that happened. No ... instead I was saying what Craig Valentine had articulated about his situation: I felt too comfortable in my good life to reach my greatest impact.

I wanted to have a bigger impact on the world around me and I wanted to do it faster.

But for now, I was comfortable … too comfortable. How did that happen? How did I (like many of us) get too comfortable in my good life? After years of dealing with challenges—the mental walls that held me back from getting to the next step—I allowed a mental box to form around me. And the thing is, this box did not feel like a jail cell; it felt more like a luxury hotel room.

This box became my new comfort zone. And every year that I stayed in it, my potential for greater impact remained farther away.

I thought back to Craig Valentine and how he broke through his box by taking action and resigning to pursue his dream of public speaking. I realized that we all need to constantly reevaluate where we are at any given time and figure out our current "quit the job" moment in order to break through our comfort zones now and get closer to where we want to be. And yes, that might actually mean quitting your job.

Taking Action NOW with Lawline

Taking action was critical to breaking through some of my largest walls at Lawline. One of my more challenging periods occurred during a six-year span where I ran through three COOs. At one point when I was on my third, Gabriel, I felt myself falling back into the same old trap: the entire company was reporting to him and I was out of the loop. We had no trust with each other and I was desperate for a solution.

When Gabriel arrived in 2014, he brought the fearlessness that I was craving. He already had helped grow a similar company. He had managed a big team. He had sales and marketing experience. And, he was super-confident in himself.

Similar to my first COO, William, he could motivate others and invest in them. I believe he applied his substantial expertise and tried his best to improve the company, but as he said to me at one point, he also felt he was sold a bill of goods when he came here. He thought our system was set up more for enterprise sales. Instead, he said he found himself at a company that discounts often, with a lack of true leadership from the top down.

The Tipping Point

Right after we hired Gabriel he said to me, "If I have not grown the company at the end of year one, then I am not the right person for the role."

I pushed back and said, "It is not solely based on growth, it is building a foundation." But as the one-year mark came, not only had sales not gone up, they had actually declined. We took some risks that did not pay off. To be honest, I was less concerned about that than the fact that Gabriel and I were not communicating properly. There was no accountability between us and no structure for checking in and discussing progress.

As we headed into our second year together, things did not improve in our relationship. It became clear that Gabriel either was going to leave on his own or I was going to ask him to leave, and once that happened, I would be exactly where I was two years earlier when COO #2, Jeff, resigned. (More on that story in Chapter 5.)

During Gabriel's tenure, I was in my second year on the board for EO, running the mentorship program. First off, I cannot tell you how important it was for me to be around like-minded individuals. Almost everyone I shared my stories with either had a similar problem with their #2 or had sometime in their past.

I decided to call my EO mentor, Ben Kirshner, and share my issues with him. Without a doubt, he knew exactly what I needed. "You need to hire a coach who can create structure and accountability in your company. There are two coaching organizations that can do this: Entrepreneur Operating System (EOS) and Verne Harnish's outfit, Gazelles."

Hearing that was like a shock to my system. "Of course!" I screamed.

Forming an Executive Team

After that call with Ben, I picked up Verne's 2015 book, *Scaling Up: How a Few Companies Make It … and Why the Rest Don't*, and after reading the first 30 pages, I could not believe the similarity I saw with what he was saying and what we were going through at Lawline. I recognized that a lot of the leadership challenges facing us were actually very common and were major contributing factors that prevented companies from scaling.

Sourcing my network in EO, I was able to find and interview a handful of Gazelles coaches and ultimately chose Mark Green from Performance Dynamics. He talked shop at the high level that I appreciated. So, I decided to get out of my comfort zone and take action. I hired him to help us find our accountability, process, and focus.

There would be one of two outcomes from this action. Either Gabriel and I would start to build a trusting relationship, or he was going to reject the process and it would speed up his departure from the company.

When Mark first started with us, he asked me to identify our company's top learners, and three people came to mind right away. The first person I thought of was my sister Michele. She is Lawline's VP of operations and has been with the company since the beginning. Her intelligence, experience with people, and administrative abilities have kept Lawline on its path to success.

Sigalle and Rich also came to mind. At the time, Sigalle had been with us for several years, and to this day has proven to be one of the smartest, driven people I know. She is always looking for the next challenge and to grow as an individual. Rich has some of the rawest talent of anyone I have ever worked with. He was a bartender before he worked at Lawline and then started in nighttime customer service, where he managed our phones by himself into the wee hours of the morning. He quickly moved to a daytime position because we recognized his talent, and before long he was again promoted, but this time to head of marketing.

Mark told me to limit the learning group to five people, so with him, Michele, Sigalle, Rich, Gabriel, and me, I knew right away we had good individuals in place. Still, I didn't fully understand at the time where he was going with it. So, I must admit I was a little surprised when, at our first meeting, he looked at us and said, "You all are now the Lawline executive team."

It was at that moment I felt vindicated because he had just empowered Rich and Sigalle to think beyond their respective roles and departments to consider the company as a whole. This had already been part of Michele's mindset from the beginning, so at this point, I knew if Gabriel left the company we would be okay.

I felt very proud of getting out of my comfort zone to take action. I had a vision, which was to protect the company and prepare myself for Gabriel's eventual departure. So, I went ahead and hired a coach and formed an executive team. Soon thereafter, Gabriel did leave the company, and it did not hit us as hard as the departures of the previous two COOs. We were now on a new path, and it felt great.

Taking Action NOW with the FFwd Mindset

I decided to write this book because I knew that I had to share what I have over learned the past 11 years. When you reach 40, you usually have had some success. You have some money saved; you're somewhat settled in your life. Yet you don't have everything you want, and you still have some bigger dreams of the impact you are going to make on the world around you. As with all dreams, you're not necessarily thinking very specifically in terms of making things happen within a certain time period. But when you're in your 40s, you suddenly realize, "If I don't start fast-forwarding my impact soon, this may never actually happen."

This book was my action step to get out of my comfort zone and share what I have learned with the FFwd Mindset in a very public and life-changing way.

Your Turn to Take Action

It is your turn to take action NOW. Start by looking back at the list of thoughts and outcomes you created in Chapter 2. If you have not yet done so, take a few moments to do it now. If you do not want to do it now, that is okay—just think of one area in your life where you want to be more fearless.

Got it? Okay, great! Now move on to the Step 1 Plan that follows this chapter, and spend five minutes answering the questions.

Okay...I know you want to skip the work. I understand, as I always want to skip it as well! So, how about this? Set a timer for five minutes, and once time is up, stop and move on. It should be quick and easy, but most importantly, *reviewing it will start to give you more energy*. Why? You are starting to see a path for how you can take action to break out of your comfort zone NOW!

STEP **1** PLAN

TAKE ACTION

Here are four **W** questions you need to ask before you take action to get out of your comfort zone.

+ **Where?**

+ **What?**

+ **Why?**

+ **When?**

Remember ... these are the four practices for getting out of your comfort zone:

+ **PRACTICE 1** – Don't Label

+ **PRACTICE 2** – Take Ownership of Your Thoughts

+ **PRACTICE 3** – Know What Makes You Special

+ **PRACTICE 4** – Take Action NOW

Are you ready to take action? Begin by answering these questions:

Where do you want to be more Fearless?

To help find the answer to this, look at the Thoughts/Actions worksheet you completed in Chapter 2. The key to success is it has to be specific enough that you can create a plan with dates and goals. If it was to "become a better leader," that might be too broad, but something like "hire a coach to help me scale my company" would work better in this context.

Research backs up the power of being specific. Psychologists Edwin Locke and Gary Latham found that when people set specific and challenging goals, it led to higher performance 90 percent of the time. They also found that the more specific and challenging the goals, the higher the motivation for hitting them.

What level out of your comfort zone is it? (1 to 10)

Going out of your comfort zone does not always have to feel like an 8 or above. Therefore, quitting your job might be way too big for you right now, but starting a seven-minute daily exercise routine might be just what you need.

Why are you doing this?

This is a great question to answer so you can constantly refer back to it when you have fear or a wall in front of you.

When will you start?

Until you attach a date to your goal, it is not a commitment. Do not feel rushed to set this date until you are ready to take action!

Write your answers to these question in a place where you can refer to them daily!

Download the template from ffwdmindset.com/resources.

STEP **1** PLAN

TAKE ACTION

There are four **W** questions you need to ask before you take action to get out of your comfort zone.

Where do you want to be more Fearless?

Hint: The more specific the better.

What level out of your comfort zone is it? (1-10)

Hint: You don't always need to feel like you are an 8 or above.

Why are you doing this?

Hint: You will need to refer to this when walls are in front of you.

When will you start?

Hint: Don't rush to get a date until you are ready.

STEP

2

NIP FEAR
IN THE BUD!

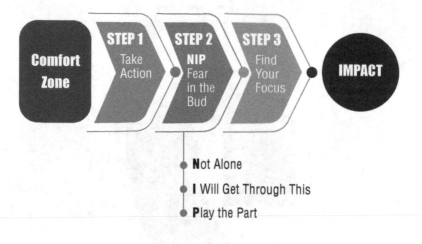

F ear is part of being an entrepreneur, and sometimes it can be overwhelming. Even after we build up the confidence to get out of our comfort zone, doubts set in on whether or not we are making the right choices.

The constant fear we face, the self-doubt, the indecision, the worry— all are universal feelings and have existed since the beginning of humanity. That is why self-help is a multibillion-dollar industry with gurus like Tony Robbins, Jack Canfield, and Mel Robbins. It is why Gary Vaynerchuk's messages about attitude and self-confidence have gotten him millions of followers on social media. We all seek solutions for how to get through our fears and self-doubts.

At the end of the day, we all want to do one thing, and that is to *NIP Fear in the Bud*, just as when you nip a flower in the bud you kill it before it can grow. In Step 2, I show you how to NIP Fear in the Bud when faced with a *wall*—a challenge or self-doubt.

Here are the main things to remember and practice in order to NIP Fear in the Bud:

N = Not Alone

You are not alone in your fear and self-doubt. Recognizing this and understanding that you are actually *in a crowd of successful entrepreneurs, all of whom face the same walls and have the same doubts,* is a key component to being fearless.

I = I Will Get Through This

Getting through each wall in front of you can be difficult and overwhelming. You won't always get to where you want to be, but that insecure feeling you face with a big wall in front of you will eventually go away. In this step, I offer four key strategies to help you through the process.

P = Play the Part

Another key practice for conquering fear is playing the part—being the best you can without being concerned about what anyone else thinks about you.

This acronym, NIP, is my "magic mantra," one that I repeat to myself all the time when I'm facing serious challenges in my business and life. Whenever I face a mental wall, I literally repeat it again and again, reprogramming my mind so that I will overcome my fear until I get through it. It never fails me, so I hope it will become your magic mantra too.

In this step, I break down each letter of NIP and circle back at the end to show how you can use this mantra day in and day out with the challenges you face in entrepreneurship and life.

5 NOT ALONE

 *14 Minutes*

As I note in Step 1, if you are confident in yourself, the world is your oyster! However, here is the key thing to understand about confidence: no one, *not one single person*, is confident or fearless all of the time.

Whenever I speak about the FFwd Mindset, I ask for a show of hands for those who are fearless 100 percent of the time. No hands go up. Then I'll say, "Raise your hands if you have moments of lack of confidence, fear of failure, and are concerned about what others think of you." Everyone's hand goes up! The message is crystal clear to anyone in the room. You are not alone.

We Share the Same Walls

The reality is that you are in a crowd of millions of passionate people who have faced the walls of entrepreneurship and you are not alone trying to FFwd your impact. Every successful person has to face the walls on a regular basis and break through them.

For every single story I share in this book, every challenge I faced, every emotional wall I confronted, I now know that I was not alone in what I went through and how it made me feel. It is this knowledge that brings me power today. Every single entrepreneur has been through similar walls or are facing them now.

Following is a list of the walls that I mention throughout this book. Put a check next to the ones that are similar to those you have faced. (I'll bet there are many.)

+ Breaking a commitment .... (Chapters 3, 9)
+ Not having confidence in your decision...................... (Chapters 5, 2)
+ Being concerned about what others think of you .... (Chapter 5)
+ Not seeing red flags until it is too late................................ (Chapter 5)
+ Being betrayed by those who work for you .... (Chapter 3)
+ Lack of focus and accountability with your team ...... (Chapters 4, 8)
+ Trouble replacing a key position.. (Chapter 4)
+ Lack of focus when executing a project .... (Chapters 4, 8)
+ Trouble handling a disrespectful employee...................... (Chapter 5)
+ Repeating the same mistakes year after year .... (Chapter 4)
+ Doing things too quickly.. (Chapters 6, 7)
+ Feeling disloyal to an employee... (Chapter 7)
+ Fear that you will lose what you have .... (Chapters 6, 7)
+ Searching for the next step....................................... (Chapters 1, 4, 5)
+ Putting off having a tough conversation .... (Chapter 5)
+ Dealing with rejection .... (Chapter 1)
+ Being disrespected by your boss....................................... (Chapter 1)
+ Feeling dissatisfied with your career .... (Chapter 1)
+ Dealing with a project taking longer than expected ..... (Chapters 5, 6)
+ Hitting the runner's walls... (Chapter 8)
+ Feeling like a fraud .... (Chapter 3)
+ Being afraid to speak in public.. (Chapter 3)
+ Getting too comfortable in your good life........................ (Chapter 4)
+ Getting the courage to quit your job to pursue a dream. (Chapter 4)

In entrepreneurship, this list can go on and on. Too often we look at our walls as bad things that are preventing us from getting where we are going. But as I point out in Step 1, a wall in front of you can also be the best thing that ever happened because of the new direction in which it will lead. *Good Thing, Bad Thing, Who Knows?*

Not Alone in the Entrepreneurs' Organization (EO)

Entrepreneurs' Organization is a peer-to-peer organization of 13,000+ leading entrepreneurs dedicated to helping each other learn and grow through once-in-a-lifetime experiences and connections to experts—those who have clocked a lot of successful mileage on the entrepreneurial path. The New York chapter, of which I am currently president (2018–2019), has about 200 members whose companies have a million dollars or more in revenue. We meet once a month, and I personally mentor a lot of entrepreneurs running smaller businesses who eventually want to join EO.

One of the things you realize when you're surrounded by all these other entrepreneurs and you start listening to them is that everybody has the same problems. That's why coaches are successful. Not because they're super smart. They just have worked with hundreds of people who say the same thing every day. There are no new problems, so the peer-to-peer mentoring is very valuable. As you can see, I am a big fan of utilizing coaches to get ahead, and I share key examples throughout this book.

You're Not Alone with Hiring and Management Problems!

Leading other people, especially your #2, is one of the most challenging things entrepreneurs go through in running and growing a business. The people issues are always the most vexing. There have been scores of books written about this topic, and Verne Harnish's *Scaling Up* contains an entire section on people. In fact, the intro of his book talks about how drama at the top of the organization leads to dysfunction in the entire company. This was my exact problem.

The primary reason I hired coach Mark Green was my realization of how common these management issues were. Up until that point, I felt alone with the problems I was having with a string of COOs as I tried to grow Lawline.

Consider the saga I describe in the following pages and let me know if it doesn't sound familiar. My stories might not compare to yours exactly, but the emotions I experienced will most likely resonate. As I mentioned in the introduction, I am a big believer in the power of sharing experience to cement a concept. That is why I am telling you all about the not-so-pretty side of being a leader and entrepreneur. My goal is to reinforce the point that we all go through the same type of stuff all the time.

Jeff: Ready, Fire, Aim

Within months of firing my first COO, William, in late 2010, one of our most talented employees, Jeff, pitched me to take over. Jeff had proven himself over the previous two years by growing from an intern to running the marketing department and managing a team of six with relative ease. He would outwork anybody he went up against. So, I promoted him to be my #2.

After he started as COO, our sales increased significantly, and Jeff continued with his outstanding work ethic to improve the company and fuel our growth. In fact, it was during this time that he single-handedly reengineered our marketing platform, leading to seven figures in additional growth within two years.

One of the things that Jeff was most proud of in his career was his "shoot first and aim second" strategy. It actually works a lot of the time because too often people get so consumed with making sure their aim is perfect that they never actually get around to shooting. That's where many of us get stuck at the walls that seem to block the way forward.

By all accounts, everything was going great except for two big components. Jeff was effectively a team of one. He was the brains behind almost all of our departments, specifically marketing and development, and there was no process in place to create institutional knowledge that all could share. There actually was no written plan, with the growth strategy existing primarily in Jeff's mind.

Second, similar to my previous COO, William, he effectively did not report to me and instead did his own thing. I provided vision and ideas every so often, but we had no regular meetings. Jeff was increasing the revenue of the company, people were reporting to him, and I did not want to get in his way. To be honest, nor did I want to spend time micromanaging his process.

The SaaS Crucible

We believed we had an opportunity in taking what we had built for Lawline and licensing it to other companies as a subscription-based software-as-a-service (SaaS) platform. As we got started on this endeavor back in 2011, we learned that it was not so easy. The entire product had to be rebuilt from the ground up. Then, *if and when* we built it in a way that would allow it to be offered to the market, we would need to hire a team to sell it.

After many months of little progress, I plopped myself down in Jeff's office to figure out a go-forward plan. "Jeff, this is taking a lot longer to build than expected. What's the big hold up?"

Jeff sighed. "We are getting close. We just have a few more kinks to work out."

"Great, that means we need to ramp up our sales and marketing strategy for getting this to market," I responded. "I am a little concerned that does not exist already, and I am frustrated that the completion date is a moving target." This conversation went on for another 30 minutes or so with me asking questions and Jeff giving answers that in my mind were not satisfactory.

The meeting came to an abrupt ending when I asked one question too many for Jeff's liking and he finally said with disdain, "This is my project. You should focus on your own things!" With that, I was caught off guard. Not wanting to go any further down this road and say something that would end in a bad place for us both, I responded "fine" and walked out of his office.

I have always struggled in these one-on-one situations. Did I say the right thing? Did I offend him? Was I strong enough? Was I logical enough? Was I decisive enough? Was I micromanaging too much, or was I practicing the right type of leadership?

In these moments I felt so alone in my doubts. *Sound familiar?*

At the end of the year, Jeff and I went out to dinner to reflect on the previous twelve months and discuss plans for the future. That is when he told me that the next year was going to be his last with the company. He shared that he felt the need to have more of an impact in the world and did not see how Lawline at that point would allow him to reach his full potential. In truth, I was surprised and definitely concerned, but I also was relieved. We had not gotten along for quite some time, and Jeff was effectively letting me off the hook by leaving.

A Last-Ditch Effort with Jeff

After some pushing from my dad, Jeff and I decided to try work out our issues so he would stay at Lawline beyond the year. The problem was that I was working out of fear of Jeff leaving versus having a truly challenging discussion on what we needed to do to fix our relationship. We needed true accountability. We needed a communication rhythm. We needed plans in writing and a commitment to see them through. I needed to have more confidence in my decisions and Jeff needed to trust them more as well. At the end of the day, not only was I not able to be fearless to make the right decisions, I lacked the focus to make our relationship work. Sound familiar?

FurtherEd: Taking Action Without Proper Planning

Taking action without proper planning is one of the most common things that entrepreneurs do, especially early on. In 2012, I changed the name of the company from Lawline to FurtherEd. We were expanding into other continuing education verticals and felt the name, Lawline, would be too limiting. My true passion and dream was, and still is, lifelong learning. So I felt by changing the name it would make it easier for things to happen.

In truth, we rushed to change the name. It was during this era of ready, fire, aim. Jeff was getting antsy and wanted to be part of something bigger than Lawline. In part, I changed the name to appease his desire for quicker growth and I justified it because it fell in line with my dream.

Changing the name was not easy logistically; it impacted our legal documents, payroll, and other systems. From a messaging standpoint, it was a mess. The other verticals never took off as we anticipated, and one by one, we shut them down. The only one that succeeded was accounting. As a result, we kept the FurtherEd name to represent our continuing professional education (CPE) product in that area.

I would leave the lifelong learning dream for another day. My dad had proven to be very cautious when stopping something. He felt that if you hold it long enough, it will eventually mature to something of value. He had proven that dozens of times with real estate and now with Lawline itself.

In Step 1, you learned the importance of building up confidence to take action regardless if you have a full plan or not. So, do not fret if my experience with FurtherEd here sounds all too familiar. This step is about how to overcome fear associated with that, and in Step 3 you'll learn how to create a focused plan. Always remember this: Even with a focused plan, the outcomes may not be what you wanted. That is part of the process. Do not label the outcomes and just keep moving forward.

"This Ends Now"

Not long after that meeting with Jeff, I decide to take my dad to an ed-tech conference in Arizona. On the plane ride back, I said to him, "Our SaaS platform in its current form will not make it. It is not built right, it does not have the team to support it, and its success is not a life-or-death situation for our business." Up until that point, my dad thought our new platform was the best thing since sliced bread. Now that he had the context, he agreed completely. With my dad's confidence on my side, I decided that putting all of our energy back into Lawline's core business would be the best chance we would have for growth.

When I got back to New York City, I shared my conclusion with Jeff. It did not go well. "So you want to kill it?" he shot back. I said, "Yes it is time." He walked out of my office and did not say another word. Up until that point, we had good momentum in our relationship. With that line, whatever goodwill we had built up the past few months was gone. And quickly, we were back to where we were before, if not worse.

Certainly, looking back at this conversation, I can see where Jeff was coming from. I collaborated with my dad as a mentor and made the decision with him, not my COO. I did not have the confidence in myself to have that conversation with Jeff or the mental tools to come up with a better plan. So it was just easier to inform him of what I thought was best at that stage.

Through email a week later, we had another disagreement about an employee. Jeff and I had many disagreements, but this time he actually crossed the line and insulted me. I responded to his email right away: "What you said can never happen again or that will be the end." It was really the first time I confronted Jeff (even though it was via email), and treated him more like an employee than as a partner.

How did he react? The next day he walked into my office with an envelope and stated, "After reading your email, I completely agree with your assessment that what I said was unacceptable. I have become someone I never want to be at work. As a result, I am giving my two weeks' notice." He handed me the envelope and walked out.

That was it. Four years of working together, one-year notice given at the end of the previous year, Jeff agreeing to stay longer, and now he was giving me two weeks' notice. Keep in mind that he had not yet started the process of detaching our marketing and development from his brain, so this was a huge deal.

After Jeff left my office, I called my dad and told him what had transpired. You could hear the fear from his silence. "Okay, I will come to the office later today and talk to him." By this time, I was done with the whole situation and said, "No, this ends now."

After that, Jeff barely lasted a week because the tension between us had become too high. He wrote letters to the entire company and gave a farewell speech. A week or so later, he mailed me a hand-written letter that was touching and went straight to the heart.

Jeff admitted something that caught me off guard. "I never really wanted to leave Lawline. In fact, I was hurt that night when I was giving you the one-year notice and instead of you being upset by it, you seemed excited and appeared to look forward to me leaving." I learned another important lesson: when someone says they want to leave, it doesn't necessarily mean they *really* mean it.

Jeff and I had a true, fond respect for each other and who we were deep inside. Over the previous twelve months, things had taken a turn for the worse, but that did not change the fact that we both held the same core values that connected us in the first place.

Not long after, I responded with my own email that hit a similar chord. If I had to be honest, while my business relationship with Jeff ended differently from that of my first COO, it was my same lack of focus and inability to be fearless when needed that ultimately killed it. With both failures I felt very alone, but instead, I should have reminded myself that this was all part of the process.

Picking Things Up After Jeff Left (2012)

As Jeff was leaving, he started to put together a budget that would allow us to cut expenses if things fell apart after he walked out the door. (They didn't.) While we didn't grow much the next 12 months, we held steady as we tried to rebuild our marketing engine.

With marketing stabilized my number one focus became finding Jeff's replacement. Unlike when I fired William and was not certain if we even needed someone in that position, now it was clear to me I needed to find someone with management experience. Between Jeff and William, I had gone almost four years without being heavily involved in the day-to-day, and here I was, thrown back into it overnight. The company was craving leadership, and I was not able to step up in the way I desired.

I was doing my best to project leadership, as I knew that is what was needed. I started to lean on my dad heavily during this time because I quickly saw that I was driving my team crazy. My mind was changing constantly about who we needed to hire, and I just wanted to talk out all sides with them. At one point, our director of HR told me the back and forth was too much for her. As soon as she thought we had a direction, she put all her energy into implementing it, only to be told by me a week later to hold off. *Sound familiar?*

Around the same time, I was approached by one of my trusted leaders in the company, Sigalle. "David, I just want to let you know I am ready and willing to move up to the COO position." I truly appreciated this and thanked her. However, after my experience with Jeff, I felt at this stage we were better off hiring someone with high-level management experience.

That led me to hire Gabriel, and when that relationship started to fail less than two years later, I decided to take action by hiring Mark Green to help bring structure, process, and accountability to the company. (I discuss this in more detail in Chapter 4.)

The biggest challenge for me during that period was recognizing early on that Gabriel was not a culture fit, and instead of dealing with it when I should have, I ignored it. In the end, my lack of clear accountability and focus was not fair to the company or to Gabriel.

When You Realize You're Not Alone

There was a startling commonality in all of these experiences: each COO felt I was holding him back from his potential. The common element in all three of these relationships was lack of *focus and accountability*. It wasn't until I started working with Mark and he provided me with tools and guidance to do this that it became clear why those relationships failed and, many times, why I got stuck at the walls in front of me.

There are different phases in any business. For the first five years at Lawline, I was the hub, and the spokes all came to me. At that phase, everything was on me, and there was a lot of pressure. Phase 2 was with three COOs in six years, and as a result, we focused on building a stronger foundation that did not revolve around me. In Phase 3, we started working with our coach to build on the foundation, and we put all our energy in setting up the company to scale. Now we are in phase 4, scaling and growing the company at record levels.

There always are going to be walls—you get past one, and there's another behind it.

During our first three phases, we faced many walls. (Spoiler alert: there would be plenty more in Phase 4 and beyond.) It's easy to feel alone when facing walls. Many times, you just want to put your head down and make the whole experience go away. It's not a comfortable place, but every entrepreneur faces these same challenges. So keep your head high. You are doing it! In Chapter 6, you'll learn four strategies to help you break through these walls and keep moving forward.

6 I WILL GET THROUGH THIS

 *17 Minutes*

I n addition to knowing you are not alone in whatever walls you face, you need to tell yourself unequivocally, "I will get through the wall in front of me." The first step in doing this is to look at your past and find examples of walls that you already have broken through. Use those as proof that you have what it takes to do it again now and in the future. It does not need to be apples-to-apples or even at the same level out of your comfort zone. The key is *remembering the feeling* that you did not think you could get through the challenge, yet you did.

In this chapter, you will learn four key strategies to help you get through your wall. First, I will share a wall we encountered at Lawline. Not only did we almost not get through it, but it almost fell right on top of us.

The Website Project that Tested Us

Have you ever plunged into a project only to find that you were *too* deep into it, overwhelmed by the decision you made, and unsure how you will get to the other end? I have, as have countless others, so you're not alone in having experienced that.

In early 2014, our lead developer at Lawline, Joe, advised us that we needed to upgrade our website. As with many other companies that start off small, our website was not built for scale. It was more like an inverted pyramid—a bad foundation to which we had added content and features year after year. That was highly inefficient.

In addition, when we built the original site, there were no frameworks we could use to make the coding easier and more stable. Our website code was known as *spaghetti code*. It did the job but was messy and very difficult to build upon.

I remember reading Eric M. Jackson's book, *The PayPal Wars*, where I learned how that company had faced a similar problem. Their website would crash often in the early days because they had millions of people flooding their servers, and their code could not handle the traffic.

For us, the issue wasn't scalability, as we had 50,000 attorneys using our site per year, not per day. Our problem was when we went to update the code to one section of the site, it would inadvertently crash another. Then, as we tried to fix it, we would cause another problem until we were simply afraid to touch any part of the site.

Joe put together a presentation so we could assess the two options of what he saw we could do next.

We met to discuss, and Joe started his speech. "Our first option is to slowly build on top of different sections of the site, which would be a big improvement over time. However, it will not allow us to rebuild the infrastructure of our database, which, if I am going to be honest, is the real problem that needs to be fixed."

Joe continued, "The second option is we rebuild the website from scratch with a new database infrastructure and a framework that will allow us to scale the website over the next ten years. However, if we choose this option we have to stop all updates and minor fixes on the existing website."

I could see that Option 2 was the right way to go, but I had serious concerns. "Joe, we are making updates and fixing bugs on the live website almost every day. How can we just stop?" Before letting Joe answer, I continued with my most important question of all: "How long will it take to rebuild the website from the ground up?"

Joe looked at me as if he had anticipated these questions and had practiced the answer a dozen times in his head. "I predict it will take six months to complete the website rebuild. In terms of your first question, I am confident the less we touch the existing website, the less we will need to do bug fixes."

With those two answers, he had my buy-in, so I said, "Let's do it!"

One Wall After Another

Luckily, Joe was right. Once we stopped touching the core site, the bugs almost came to a halt, so we did not need to focus our energy on that.

However, those six months turned into just over two years. During that time, one by one, each member of Joe's three-person development team left. One went to a dream job to teach code. Another moved across the country. The third technically quit but stayed on as a contractor to help us see the launch through and continues to contribute for user interface design to this day. Instead of hiring a new in-house team, we decided to put our energy into hiring an outsourced team to support Joe, but those efforts failed and it ended up wasting a lot of time.

As the weeks and months passed amid ongoing challenges and a constantly changing development-team environment, Joe continued to put all of his energy into finishing the new site. If anyone could do it, he could ... but I could also tell that the pressure was starting to get to him.

"Guys, I have decided to resign."

One day, in September 2015, Joe had finally reached his breaking point too.

He asked to sit down with Gabriel and me in the conference room. From my years of experience, that is never a good sign. "Guys, I have decided to resign. However, I want to give plenty of notice as to what I expect from my team. So, I will stay on for three months while you find someone and train them to replace me." While I was very grateful for the long lead time, I knew it would not be enough for us to find someone to replace him or finish the site.

By that time, Joe and I had become rather close since he had been at Lawline for four years. We took a walk the next day to discuss his decision.

He was straightforward. "David, over the previous six months I have felt my health deteriorating. I have been sleeping less, and my stress level is too high. As important as the site is to me, I have to protect myself first."

After hearing this, I had no fight left in me. I told him, "I totally understand your health is the most important thing. Do not to worry about us. We will get through it."

However, inside I was not as confident. The new website challenge had directly taken out three people on the dev team, and it was about to take Joe out as well. It was a big wall—larger than we ever had imagined at the outset. Increasingly, not only did it look like we couldn't break through the wall, it looked as if it was going to fall down on us.

Stalled at the 10-Yard Line

Early the next week, Gabriel and I sat down to discuss the situation. Gabriel was pretty strong-willed about his opinion: "If Joe completes this project, it will be the most rewarding achievement of his career. We are essentially at the 10-yard line, and to quit now will be demoralizing for him and for us." I never thought about it before in terms of Joe's career accomplishment, and Gabriel was completely right. Joe breaking this commitment to finish the website would make him feel better now but would probably bother him for the rest of his career.

I continued with the football analogy. "The main issue is the final 10 yards are not getting shorter. Every time Joe crosses off five things on his list, seven new ones get added." Gabriel nodded in complete agreement. I stated, "In order to get the new website live, we are going to need to cut our website wish list in half and then in half again and keep cutting until we get to the bare essentials."

Gabriel thought about this for a while and summarized this situation perfectly. "If Joe stays an additional three months on top of the three-months' notice he already gave us, that would be more than enough to launch the new website and find a replacement." At the end of the day, he said, "Three months is not a long time to him, but it would mean the world for the business."

Gabriel decided to talk to Joe and share his feelings. Then Joe and I talked about his mental health, as well as whether we possibly could extend his notice to six months. After a long conversation, he came back to me the next day and said, "I am in. I will stay for six months until we launch the website." We came up with a plan that would give priority to his quality-of-life concerns and compensate him for his time.

Two important members of the soon-to-be-created executive team were an important part of this plan. Rich took ownership to manage the daily project planning, so all Joe had to focus on was coding. Michele took ownership over hiring, so Joe only needed to get involved when we had a very qualified candidate. And Joe would not work nights or weekends, which he had been doing the previous months.

I thought we had a pretty good plan. Rich went into action and started cutting the site requirements right away. We set a hard-stop completion date at the end of March when Joe was to go on a two-week vacation to Israel.

For the next several weeks, everything went well. We hired three great developers to work with Joe. We were rebuilding the team and finalizing the site. But the March 31 date was fast approaching. We moved off of the 10-yard line, but now we were stuck on the 3.

Because of the hard stop, Joe once again started working nights and weekends to hit the deadline.

Zero Hour and Decision Time

It was late March 2016. We finally were at zero hour, but we weren't done and had to make a decision. Rich was going to India for two weeks and Joe would be in Israel. We were close, but launching the site with both of them gone while the final punch list was incomplete could be a disaster.

The entire development team joined Rich and me in a conference room to decide if we were going to launch the new website. I was nervous because it seemed to be shaping up as a lose-lose situation. Either we would launch the website before they both left on their trips, risking disaster, or we would wait, risking the possibility that Joe would decline to work any longer past his hard-stop deadline.

Rich has always excelled at telling it like it is. Looking at the list of issues on the new site, he stated in a matter-of-fact voice, "Okay, we cannot go live. We will have to wait until we get back." Rich had to know what the consequences could have meant with Joe saying he was leaving, but Rich said it in a way that indicated it really was our only option.

The meeting ended and Joe and I stayed in the conference room. "Dave, I am done," he told me. "I have put every ounce of energy into the website. I have stayed up nights and worked weekends the past few weeks to get us here. I cannot do this any longer."

Joe was on the verge of crying, and to be honest, I was as well. I felt responsible for the state of his health. We talked for a few minutes and finally I said, "Joe, I am so sorry. You have done what you promised. You are right. Enough is enough. We will find a way to get this live without you. Thank you for everything." I felt like I was tearing up, so I just ended the conversation.

A weird thing happened at that moment. Joe did not expect me to get as distraught as I did. He knew it was affecting him, but he was not trying to get *me* so emotional. So, he calmed the situation down.

He said, "Let's both take a day or two to refresh and reboot. I am not going to think about the website. Once I have a fresh mind, I will come up with a plan of what the best next steps are for me." I agreed and we did not talk for the next two days.

He came back with a plan that made sense, and this time a hard stop really would be the end of his involvement—win, lose, or draw. It was fair and I truly appreciated it.

Joe went off on his vacation and would jump back into the project two weeks later when he got back. It turned out there was a benefit to this in that it gave the new development team an opportunity to be responsible for the website without Joe as a backup. They did great, and I also believe that it gave them the confidence that everything would be fine when Joe finally left Lawline.

During this time, we once again cut down the launch list to essentials only. Any "nice to haves" would have to wait until Phase 2. When Joe and Rich came back from their respective vacations, we hit the ground running.

Breaking Through the Wall

Within six weeks, we were as launch-ready as we would ever be. The entire development team and I came into the office on a Saturday and we got to work.

Joe had named the launch of the new site "Austin" in deference to Steve Austin, the main character from the television series, *The Six Million Dollar Man*, because he was rebuilt stronger and faster. On the day of the launch, he even gave each of us a little action figure of the Six Million Dollar Man with a button on it that played the theme song of the show. I still have it on my desk!

The actual switchover to the new website was fairly easy. We simply needed to point the Lawline.com domain to the new server. Once that was done, we immediately went to work to find any undiscovered bugs that you don't see until the website is in the live environment. We found a few and fixed them within a couple of hours.

Success! We broke through the wall! We all paused to celebrate. I had brought a bottle of Basil Hayden's whiskey (Joe's favorite) to celebrate the occasion. I opened up the bottle, and we finished it in record time. It was a critical day for our company and for Joe. It set a secure foundation for our growth for the next 10 years and became Joe's crowning achievement at that point in his career.

Throughout this incredibly daunting task, we believed in ourselves and kept pushing, and we got through it.

As life would have it, Joe and I have continued to stay close since he left. As a matter of fact, he has started his own company and we became his first client.

Four Mental Strategies for Getting Through It

Telling yourself, "I will get through this" is an important affirmation that builds confidence and resilience to make what you are saying become a reality. In fact, affirmations have helped thousands of people make significant changes in their lives, according to Ronald Alexander PhD, a licensed psychotherapist, leadership consultant, clinical trainer, and author of *Wise Mind, Open Mind.*

In addition to repeating this affirmation, there are four mental strategy tools you can use to help you be more fearless as you face walls in front of you. These are designed to be used at the drop of a hat. When you are experiencing fear, do one or more of the following and you will feel it start to dissipate.

1. Fill Your Bucket

How Full is Your Bucket? by Tom Rath and Donald O. Clifton began as a children's book, then was modified into an edition for professionals, focusing on the same topic. This book explains that we all have these proverbial buckets that we carry around with us. We all walk around with a dipper that we can use either to take away from other people's buckets or fill them.

You fill people's buckets by giving them consistent, positive feedback when they are doing things well. It can be small and to the point, such as, "Great presentation this morning. You touched on all the major themes we discussed!"

I once read an article that advised readers to put 10 pennies in their right pocket. The goal was to give 10 compliments that day, and every time you did so, you could move one penny from the right pocket to the left. So I gave it a try. I spent the day giving people real compliments, but I was doing it for the exercise. Inside, I felt like a fake but carried on anyway. Then something great happened. With each compliment I gave, it led to the other person smiling, thanking me, and truly getting a sense of pride. I cannot tell you the energy it brought me by the end of the day, helping me to get through my walls.

A key component to breaking through your wall is making sure that your bucket is full. What do you think is the number one way to fill your own bucket? STOP READING. WRITE YOUR GUESS BELOW (if you want).

_____

_____

_____

_____

_____

Most people do not correctly answer this question. However, I gave you a hint in the paragraph above. *The best way to fill your bucket is to fill other people's buckets.* When you give someone a compliment, or right before you do, you feel energized and excited because you know that it is going to make them feel better. Isn't that cool? By filling other people's buckets you fill your own.

The best way to fill your bucket is to fill other people's buckets.

And the more you fill other people's buckets over time, the easier it is for them to trust your critical feedback and candor when you see areas in which they can improve. In addition, it provides you with the positive energy needed to tackle the mental walls in front of you.

2. Go 21 Days Without Complaining

I originally learned about the book *A Complaint Free World* by Will Bowen from an article written by Tim Ferriss, author of *The 4-Hour Workweek*. The goal is to go 21 days in a row without making one verbal complaint. The trick is every time you complain, you need to start over from Day 1. Similar to the switching pennies from the right to left pocket, you wear a wristband on one arm and switch it to the other every time you complain.

I tackled this exercise with optimism and energy. Until you do this, you do not realize how often you actually complain. "The weather sucks." Start over. "This traffic is so frustrating." Start over. "Michael's presentation was so boring." Start Over. "I am so out of shape." Start over. You get the drift?

I switched the bracelet probably a few dozen times the first few days. Even so, I slowly started feeling myself starting to complain less. Stuck in traffic. So what? Hold it in. Too hot outside? Oh well, no need to complain about it. The presentation was boring. Okay, no problem; just give him feedback to improve it.

As a result of this practice, I felt better about myself, and no doubt people started to look at me differently.

The less you complain, the less negative you are. The less negative you are, the more *positive* you become. The more positive you become, the easier it will be to break through the mental walls that appear in front of you. You can't complain about them; rather, you need to accept them and find solutions. I am not saying it is easy, but the concept itself is simple enough to try.

For my part, I did this for over a month, and the furthest I got was Day 8 before I had to start over again. I decided to take a break from the experiment at that stage. Maybe, at some point I will give it another go. However, it had the intended effect on me. While I still complain, I am much more cognizant of it and have reduced it significantly since before I went through this process.

Here is a great analogy about the power of complaining over time. There is a paint store in Alexandria, Indiana, that hung a baseball from the ceiling in 1977, and since then, every time someone walks in, they take a brush and put a coat of paint on it. After all of these years of people painting one coat of paint on the baseball, how much do you think it weighs?

+ 100 pounds?
+ 300 pounds?
+ 500 pounds?

Nope. It weighs *3,500 pounds!* While each coat of paint in itself did not weight much, cumulatively, over time, all of those countless layers amounted to more than a ton. It is the same thing with complaints. While each one is not that big of a deal, after years and years of complaining, they weigh you down.

Photo: Steven Pierson © 2015

The world's largest ball of paint hangs in Alexandria, Indiana, and began with a baseball hung from the ceiling on January 1, 1977.

Reducing your complaints is one of the more powerful things you can do to give yourself the confidence to break through the wall in front of you!

3. Show Gratitude for 90 Days

In 2015, my buddy Kyle and I started an email chain that turned into something much bigger than either of us could have imagined. You have no doubt read about the importance of gratitude in being a successful entrepreneur. So, we both decided to give it a go and see what would happen if we practiced gratitude daily. Kyle would email me five things for which he was grateful, and I would respond with my own five things. We could not repeat the same thing twice. So, for example, I could only be grateful for my wife once during the 30 days. However, if I went to the gym daily, I could be grateful for that each day, because it was a new action.

After the 30 days, I put all of my posts in a spreadsheet because I wanted to find the themes of what I was most grateful for. I then wrote an article for *Forbes* to share my results. (You can read it at ffwdmindset.com/resources.)

I also posted the article on Facebook, where two entrepreneurs I know saw it and had an idea to turn it into something bigger.

The four of us got together and decided to make a Facebook challenge called 90 Days to Gratitude. Could you be grateful for 90 days in a row in the same manner in which Kyle and I did it? This time, instead of just emailing it to one person, you would post it publicly in the group. We put it up, and within a few weeks, thousands of people were in the group (including my wife), and the challenge was underway.

Doing this with my wife and colleagues was so energizing! It helped cement gratitude as part of my core beliefs moving forward. My recommendation is to do a 30-day challenge with a colleague like Kyle, then join the group (it still exists), and give the 90-day challenge a go!

The bottom line is if you are grateful for what you have when a wall is in front of you, it will help reduce your worry or stress. In the same way you can't smile and frown at the same time, you can't be grateful and worried at the same moment. That will help you get through the wall in front of you.

4. Dedicate Yourself to Journaling

Journaling is another way to get through whatever challenges you face, and has been my secret weapon for years. It truly comes in handy during times of crisis when you have walls in front of you and your stress level is high. Many times I am stressed and I don't even know exactly why. That is where journaling comes into play. For me, this practice has led to lots of breakthroughs as I faced the walls in front of me.

Journaling is like exercise for your mind. When you work out physically at a gym, it breaks down your muscles and rebuilds bigger and stronger ones; journaling does this for your mind. By sitting down and recapping the day before, or writing out some issues you are facing, you are literally making new connections of neurons in your brain that are making you smarter. In fact, studies have shown that the amygdala, an almond-shaped collection of neurons inside each cerebral hemisphere of your brain, regulates your *fight-or-flight* response, processing information around you to determine whether you are in a dangerous situation. Once journaling becomes a daily habit, the amygdala begins to recognize journaling as a safe zone for personal growth. With the amygdala working with, instead of against you, you're able to grow faster and handle your challenges better.

If you practice journaling each morning, you will think on your feet more quickly, have more confidence in yourself, and most importantly, you will have less stress. Hands down, journaling is the simplest thing you can do for yourself to get through some of the tougher times in entrepreneurship.

Kim Ades has tapped into this powerful practice. She reads her clients' journals every day for 10 weeks, giving them candid feedback (as she did for me). If you want to become more fearless when facing your walls, go through that process with one of Kim's coaches at Frame of Mind Coaching. It could be transformational, as it was for me. For a free assessment, go to ffwdminset.com/resources.

I wrote in a physical journal for years before switching to an online journal format, which has several advantages. It allows others to comment, but it also makes it easier to find older entries, which I did when researching and writing this book. Penzu is an online journal that emails you the first few sentences from that date's entry for the previous year(s). It is amazing to see where the ways you think are still the same and where they have changed over time.

I do not journal every day anymore. However, when I do have a wall in front of me and I am unsure of how to get through, I go right to the journal and start brain dumping my thoughts. It might not get you through the wall, but it will help reduce worry.

You Will Get Through This

Whenever you're facing challenges, remember the affirmation "I will get through this." The four strategies will help you do that.

I have been down this same road before and learned a lot. Like you, I have done many challenging things over my life, from building my business to running marathons, to being a father of three. I have hired several experts and coaches over the years to assist me in making sure Lawline was a success, and I have grown as a leader.

I have followed the practices described in this chapter. I have reinvented the management structure of my business several times, and I will do it again as we continue to evolve.

In order to have the impact I desired, I chose to go and do something HARD, facing it head-on versus NOT doing anything, which I know would not get me anywhere. I had an entrepreneur TV show in law school as my commitment to sharing and teaching entrepreneurship and this book was a necessary next extension to that. So it has been hard, long, and challenging. I wouldn't have it any other way.

There still are walls in front of me, but like you, I will get through them. No doubt! In the next chapter, you'll learn how to maximize that effort by Playing the Part: making a decision and taking action without concern for what anyone thinks of you.

7 PLAY THE PART

 *12 Minutes*

t happens every day. Most of us tend to be concerned about what others think of us. Their opinions of us seep into our minds in one form or another.

It is natural and human to want others' approval or affirmation for what we are doing. That is why filling buckets is so important; it reinforces the positive energy people want from others. On the flip side, if someone we respect disapproves of something we are doing, it can be debilitating, leading to stress, anxiety, and self-doubt.

There is no tougher critic to overcome than a parent who does not believe in you or who doubts what you are doing. I learned this back in 2006 when I was interviewing entrepreneurs for my TV show, TrueNYC. One of the major lessons for me was *don't listen to the negativity of naysayers*. More often than not for young entrepreneurs, the most influential naysayers are parents trying to protect them from harm. Or, they project their own worries onto them.

When you are receiving negative feedback from someone, the first question you need to ask yourself is "Has this person been through what I am going through?" If that is, in fact, the case (as it has been for my dad), then you will weigh their opinion differently from someone speaking based on their own fears. As an entrepreneur, your job is to listen to everyone's feedback and make your own decision. To Play the Part means making a decision or taking action without concern for what anyone thinks of you.

Let's face it: That is hard to do as an entrepreneur, so becoming more self-assured and confident in your decision-making is important. You need to believe in yourself first and foremost! Then you need to NIP Fear in the Bud when you have self-doubt about the action you just took. This is what Steps 1 and 2 are about.

This chapter features excerpts from the actual journals I created when working with Kim Ades, along with her responses to them. It was through one of her responses that I first learned the power of Playing the Part. Using this simple concept has allowed me to get out of my comfort zone more often, and now I hope it will do the same for you.

My "Brilliant" Idea: TrueStartups

In 2012, Lawline was on pace to surpass $5 million in revenue and I was feeling on top of the world. I decided it was time to pursue my original dream to help entrepreneurs grow their businesses. I felt overly confident that since I had grown Lawline quickly, I could easily do the same with whatever I put energy into.

I convinced Kyle, our director of programming who was responsible for creating all of our legal content, to leave his day job at Lawline and do this with me. He probably assumed since I proposed the idea, I had put a lot more thought and energy into it than the few hours I'd actually dedicated to it. Heck, he might have thought I even had a *written plan*. So just like when I asked him if he would run the marathon with me, Kyle said, "Of course, let's go!" (More on our marathon journey in Chapter 8.)

I went from the highest of highs to the lowest of lows in a matter of two weeks before I shut this new venture down and retreated back to my comfort zone. The journaling started the first day that Kyle and I arrived at the coworking space with no plan. Our goal was to come up with an idea and start the business the very next week.

Journal 1 (Day 1) – Finding the Idea

One thing that became clear to me is there will NEVER be an ah-ha moment at this stage. You either copy some idea that exists and the main issue will be your "competition" or you go a new route and believe your new idea, such as a "YouTube" concept, will work. It all comes from your belief in yourself and your idea.

Our brilliant idea: a school. That did not come easily but was clear to us before noon.

Journal 2 (Day 2) – Breaking through the Wall

The day started off with Kyle and me trying to come up with what our entrepreneur school would be. After many hours, we both got frustrated that there were no clear answers, and we needed a change of scenery. We were near a small park, so we started walking around the loop. One lap turned to two, which eventually turned into 20.

I was being negative and not offering answers – just asking a lot of questions in a self-defeatist tone, such as "How are we going to get people to come? How are we going to differentiate ourselves? How are we going to make money? How are we going to start it?" How, How, How???

At one point Kyle just stopped walking and said, "You know what? We already work at a great company. If you do not think this can happen and don't want to do it, let's just stop this now and go back to Lawline tomorrow."

All of a sudden I felt like we were on our 15-mile run during our marathon-training days. At mile 8 of training for the New York City Marathon, my knee was killing me and we had to stop to get Advil. The next portion of the route went over the 59th

Street Bridge into Queens. I kept saying, "I can't do it. The hill is going to kill me on the bridge." Queens was an unknown, and what if my knee just gave out? We would be somewhere unfamiliar. I can't, I can't, I can't.

Then finally Kyle said, "Fine, then let's not do it. Let's go back the way we came." That way was safe. It was familiar.

As soon as he said, "LET'S STOP," it was a complete 180 in my mind. "I AM NOT STOPPING," I screamed. "We are going over the bridge until my knee falls off." That was the unknown, the adventure, the path we had planned in the morning. Luckily, the Advil kicked in by then and while I was still in a bit of pain, we had an AMAZING run the rest of the way.

My mind snapped back to the here and now. We were still in the park. After we sat down on the bench, I declared to Kyle, "We are not going back!" The way I said it was with such belief: I felt like I was going to cry. Not out of sadness or happiness but just out of raw emotion.

Kyle responded, "We are going to have to go forward with blind faith that this will work out. We will never have all the answers, but we have to focus on what is going well and not on the walls in front of us." We both agreed and the energy picked up right away.

Journal 3 (Day 7) – My Dad Not Believing in My Idea

My dad just came back after three weeks away and saw us in a new office, with me focusing all of my energy on this new company. He gave me such a look of disbelief and then he said, "Aren't you guys moving a little too fast? Last week you came up with a concept, announced it to the company on Friday, have a website ready today, and are now announcing it to the 'world' tomorrow?"

When I heard that, it certainly gave me pause. As I said to Kyle (probably more talking to myself), "At the end of the day, a parent does not want you to take risks and get hurt. If you do something they wouldn't have done, they try to hold you back."

My dad has been the most motivational person in my adult life (my childhood motivation award goes to my mom), but just like any parent, he has expressed doubts over the years. He originally told me I would not get into George Washington University. Then, when I worked through multiple sales positions, he told me he was concerned about my future career. Then, when I was starting Lawline with no job in sight, he told me he thought the chances of success were very low.

There is nothing that will mess with your head more than a family member, especially your dad, looking at you like you are doing the wrong thing. In the state I was in at the time, it only took one sentence from my dad to make it clear to me we were headed down the wrong path. It wouldn't have messed with me as much if I had a clearer plan of attack at the moment.

I am amazed by the peaks and valleys I have been going through over the past few days. On one hand, it catches me off guard. On the other, I know to expect it. Kyle, for better or worse, completely plays off my emotions. Every so often, he has a moment of reflection where he can get me back on track if I stray, but the rest of the time it is the former.

Coach's Response

Kim:

I am really interested in your dad's impact on your decision-making and on your psyche. He seems to yield a great deal of power. What is that about? What does he know that you don't? What is it about him that enables him to boost you up and cause such self-doubt all at the same time?

David:

Simple. His confidence in himself. Also, he is smart and has excelled in business and in life. As he says, "experience." And the power a father has over his son ... wow ... . I'll have to remember that with my kids.

Kim:

Does his confidence that this will not work reduce your own that it will?

David:

Seems to be the case … . :(

I still looked to others' perceptions of me to get their approval of my thoughts and ideas.

Journal 4 (Day 10) – My Dad Not Believing in My Idea

So let me start with my feeling right now. Fear. Fear over how easily and how fast I got stressed over the past two weeks. If I have this fear now, how can I handle much bigger situations? Am I a one-hit wonder? What if Lawline was not around or went out of business? Fear. This situation causes you to doubt yourself of course.

However, I know these are only moments of fear. With a clear head, I have full confidence in myself. At the end of the day, it does come down to having more of a plan than just an idea.

I am less concerned that we did this too fast and more about what it did to me. The main reason I got so out of whack is being next to Kyle this whole time since he would essentially amplify my anxiety with his own fears.

This was the point when I realized I still looked to others' perceptions of me to get their approval of my thoughts and ideas. When Kyle or my dad did not give positive feedback about them, it made me doubt their worth.

Why? I don't want people not to like me or believe in me. Plus, to some extent, I want approval of my concept. And what that comes down to is not enough belief in my idea on its own. The thing is no one knows what is right or wrong; you just do the best you can.

Coach's Response

Kim:

As for this running theme about what people think of you ... How would you behave if everyone thought of you as a moron? Alternately, how would you behave if everyone thought of you as a genius? What's the real truth? What DO people think of you?

David:

If everyone thought I was a moron, it wouldn't bother me because I would know they were wrong. If everyone thought I was a genius, it would energize me and I would play the part.

YOU KNOW WHAT? This made me realize that the issue is my own self-projection. So when I am unsure about why I feel a certain way, that is when I open myself up to how other people "think" of me and end up using their frame of mind, or at least what I can tell from their facial expressions, instead of mine.

"How would you behave if everyone thought of you as a moron?"

Kim:

Why can't you just Play the Part all the time? Here's the funny thing ... YOU get to decide who you are and how to show up. What you focus on grows ... focus on trusting yourself and allowing your genius to just shine through.

Journal 5 (Day 11) – It Begins with How I Think and Feel

There is a great line in The Success Principles that goes like this: At 20 you are concerned with what everyone thinks about you, at 40 you don't care what everyone thinks about you, and at 60 you realize no one was thinking about you all along as they are too busy thinking about themselves.

The past two weeks were like being in a mental-toughness school. Call it Phase I of the school. The experience for each person is different. My experience taught me the following:

1) When I am in a state of uncertainty and anxiety, I need to be on my own. I need to only care about me and my thoughts and feelings. That is it. And by this, I mean physically be alone.

2) I need to do a lot more thinking and writing before I get someone else involved in a new idea. If I have a better plan and focus, I can have more confidence in my actions.

3) If something like this happens again, which it will because that is part of the growth, I will be ready for it. I need to block and tackle and work my best to get through it. The important thing is to focus on how I THINK and I FEEL ... My thoughts lead to my beliefs, which lead to my actions, which lead to my results ...

Every fear comes down to supporting your family, mortgage, school, living, comfortable lifestyle, etc., etc. Those are things that can prevent you from not wanting to get uncomfortable again.

Coach's Response

Kim:

What is it that creates insecurity for you? Is it the uncertainty? Is it the pressure of what other people will think if you come up empty? What is it?

David:

First, is not to lose what I have. I enjoy my life, and I realize that. I also realize that getting to the next economic level will take a lot of work. Additionally, 1) I'm not sure how to take the next step, 2) I'm afraid to lose it all, 3) I want to be loyal and inspire others along the way.

Journal 6 (Day 14) – Taking Care of My Own Well-Being First

Kyle is still in a vulnerable state after I decided to shut this down. I realize I have to stop focusing on him and put all the focus on me. If I am not in the right state, he will never be. My happiness is first, or I can't help someone else. I sort of feel like I have abandoned him, and I am sure he feels that way too. I believe in the long run, though, it will be looked at as an important part of the process for making this work and getting us both to the next step.

Coach's Response:

Kim:

YES!!! Taking care of your own well-being first is always the most important thing to do. It's just like being on a plane and putting on your oxygen mask before helping others.

Reflection

Reflecting on the two weeks of TrueStartups, I realized after the ideation stage I should have dedicated a few months to create a plan, instead of trying to execute right away without clear direction. But the mental damage was done and I needed a break. I decided to stop this venture and went back into my comfort zone being CEO of Lawline. I put Kyle in a new entrepreneurial role there and did my best to salvage the situation.

The truth is that he never recovered and left the company within the year. While we were both disappointed in the way it ended, it has made our relationship stronger. Within two years of leaving, he did pursue his dream and started his own business.

Without a plan in place, the doubts from my father led me to question myself and what I was doing. Kyle's fear led me to be more fearful because I was trying to get my fearlessness from his belief in me and my ideas.

When I realized the issue was not what my dad or what Kyle thought of me, but what I thought of myself, it was a light bulb moment. Why did I need Kyle to affirm my ideas? Because I didn't have confidence in them myself. Likewise, I did not want my dad to doubt my ideas because I did not have focus on what I was doing.

When Kim asked me "why not Play the Part of a genius all the time?" it became clear that it was what I needed to do to have real impact. I needed to Play the Part as the actor onstage, concerned with giving the best performance of his lifetime versus only being concerned with how the crowd thinks he is doing.

STEP **2** PLAN

THE MAGIC MANTRA

The moment you step outside of your comfort zone, fear sets in and tries to push you back. In this section, you learned how to NIP Fear in the Bud so that you will not be pushed back into your comfort zone.

The Magic Mantra

At the beginning of Step 2, I mention a magic mantra that I say to myself when I am facing a wall. I either repeat this general statement over and over again:

"I will NIP Fear in the Bud!"

... or, I fill in the details of NIP to make it more specific to the actual wall I am facing:

"I am **N**ot alone in _____. **I** will get through it by **P**laying the part of a fearless _____."

Examples:
"I am not alone in _starting a business without a plan_. I will get through it by playing the part of a fearless _entrepreneur_."

"I am not alone in _being concerned about what my father thinks of me._ I will get through it by playing the part of a fearless _son._"

"I am not alone in _feeling like I was not loyal to someone important to me._ I will get through it by playing the part of a fearless _leader._"

To flesh out this mantra, you will find it helpful to answer the following four questions. (To see example answers and download a template, visit ffwdmindset.com/resources.)

What is Your Number One Fear in This Situation?

Once you write down your number one fear, it does not seem so intimidating anymore. Then you will go through the process to NIP that number one fear in the Bud. I also recommend doing Dale Carnegie's worst-case scenario (see Chapter 2).

Not alone (Who else is going through this?):

Lots of other people also are experiencing your number one fear or have done so in the past. Think about this and name as many people you know of who are going through or *have* gone through this at one time.

I will get through it (Past experience shows you have what it takes):

You have already accomplished a lot in your life. What are some examples of things that you have accomplished that show you can overcome this number one fear so that you can reach this goal?

Play the part (Why you are fearless and do not care about what others think):

You need to reaffirm that yours is the only opinion that matters. Write down the names of other people who might have a negative opinion of this and why that does not matter.

STEP **2** PLAN

THE MAGIC MANTRA

"I am **N**ot alone in_____.
I will get through it by **P**laying the
Part of a fearless _____."

What is your #1 fear in this situation?	**N**ot alone. Who else is going through this?
I will get through it. Past experiences that show you have what it takes.	**P**lay the Part. Why you are fearless and don't care what others think.

STEP

3

FIND YOUR FOCUS

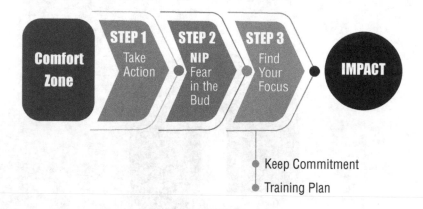

F*ocus* is a challenge faced by nearly every single person I know professionally, even if they don't know it. That's because we all fight inertia—the desire to simply be comfortable every single day in our professional lives—instead of pushing ourselves outside of our comfort zones to do more and *having the focus to stay outside* of those comfort zones to take it even further.

Throughout my entrepreneurial career, I've found that taking action to break out and stay out of my comfort zone has helped me take new risks, but too often I still would get stuck at a certain level of success and become comfortable again. There is a lot of information out there on the importance of breaking out of your comfort zone, but there is less information about why *so many people cannot stay out of it longer.* That is the trick. Falling back into your comfort zone will slow you down from having a bigger impact on yourself and others.

Step 3: Find Your Focus

Simply put, Step 3 shows you how to find the *focus* to stay out of your comfort zone longer. The longer you stay out of your comfort zone, the larger your comfort zone becomes. The larger your comfort zone becomes, the faster you do and experience more things. The more you do and experience, the more momentum you will have to create the impact you desire on the world around you!

8 KEEP YOUR COMMITMENT

 *9 Minutes*

For most of my life, the thought of running a marathon had never crossed my mind. While growing up, I witnessed my dad finish 15 marathons, and was very proud of him, but I thought it was the *last thing* I would ever want to do.

However, that changed overnight on May 5, 2011, after I first read *The Success Principles*. As I previously mentioned, the book immediately had a tremendous impact on me, but it was Principle 54, "Keep Your Agreements," that really hit home.

In this principle, Jack Canfield breaks down the internal and external consequences of breaking agreements. You start losing confidence because you find yourself less reliable, and just as importantly, so do others. He talked about how easily people break agreements. Many even know they are going to break them when they agree to them.

One example he brings up is that students who attend his class must sign an agreement not to come late. Inevitably, several people show up late a few days after the class begins, and he tells them they broke the agreement. One person says, "I can't control traffic. That is not fair."

Jack says, "If I told you that if you showed up late your loved one would be killed, would you still say that?"

The person responds, "Well if that was the case, I would never leave!" While this is obviously an extreme scenario, the question is designed to wake you up to thinking about how much further you can push yourself to keep all the agreements you make to yourself and others. This resonated with me because, at the time, I was definitely taking the approach that things were *out of my control, not my fault,* or that others *would just understand* when I broke an agreement.

Making Commitments

Of course, keeping your agreement and *making a commitment* go hand in hand. So, with Jack's example in mind, I recognized three particular areas of personal behavior that I wanted to change, and I committed myself to doing so. First, I stopped canceling meetings 10 minutes before the start time because I felt too "busy." I previously had thought my employees would understand because I am the CEO and had a lot on my plate. Now, instead of hiding behind that excuse, they are my priority.

Second, when I said I was going to do the dishes at home, *I did them.* While that might sound small, I cannot tell you how big it was for me. I adopted the new mindset of "I love my wife and will keep my commitment," as opposed to the old "My wife loves me so she will understand."

The third area was exercise. Almost everyone can relate to the nagging feeling that they are not doing enough to stay in shape. With three-year-old twins at home, I was certainly not taking care of myself and I wanted it to change. So, I gave some thought to "What is the scariest thing I could commit to?" and right away, running a marathon popped into my head.

My mindset was if I could commit to *that* and complete it after never running more than a 5K at one time, then I could do *anything* if I committed to it. The secret, of course, is treating a commitment as if your child's life was on the line versus something you can't control. The following marathon stories will show you how my commitment was put to the test time and time again and how keeping my agreement got me across the finish line each time.

Running the Philadelphia Marathon

My marathon commitment began one day when I looked at Kyle and half-jokingly said, "If I buy us tickets for the Philadelphia Marathon, will you run it with me?"

Even though at that point he only had one marathon under his belt, which had not gone well, he looked at me and smiled and said, "Let's do it." With that, I bought the tickets and the agreement was made!

Kyle and I trained for months, at all hours and in all kinds of weather. Fortunately, we had a proven marathon-training plan that I had downloaded. We followed that rigorously, no matter how uncomfortable or even how painful it got. It gave us the structure and motivation we needed to be accountable to ourselves and to each other. It prepared us for the test that was to come. (Read more about the value of a training plan in Chapter 9.)

Hitting the Wall in Philadelphia

When the big day finally arrived, Kyle and I got up before dawn and assembled with thousands of others at the starting line. The gun sounded, and we were off! During most of the marathon my training paid off and I felt great. However, marathon training is only for the first 20 miles, so during the actual race, you are basically on your own for the last six. Sure enough, it was after mile 20 that my body started to feel physically exhausted. I kept pushing, but it was not cooperating.

Many first-time marathoners know that at some point during those last six miles your body is in so much pain that it keeps sending you signals to stop. For me, it started with my feet. Every step that I took felt like I was running on broken glass, and my feet were literally burning when they touched the ground. Lactic acid had built up in the muscles of my legs, making it very difficult to move them forward. It was almost as if they were screaming at me, "STOP running!"

As I reached mile 23, the pain was immense. I badly wanted to stop even though I was "only" three miles away from keeping the hardest commitment I had ever made. I remember glancing over at Kyle, and he looked as though he had not even started yet. In fact, he was running backward and screaming at me. "Come on! You can do this! You are not going to fail!"

Step by step, mile by mile, there he was screaming at me up until I reached the finish line. (See the accompanying photo.) When I crossed, I was on the verge of collapsing from mental and physical exhaustion.

I felt like a champion. I kept my commitment!

I did it! I did it! I broke through the wall. I was ecstatic inside. I had proven to myself that with an agreement, a commitment, and a plan, I could go further and achieve more than I ever thought possible.

The New York City Marathon and Hurricane Sandy

After the high of finishing in Philadelphia, I knew I had to run the New York City Marathon and I made a new commitment. Because the New York City Marathon is world-renowned and incredibly popular, most people who are not world-class runners need to

*When I finished the Philadelphia Marathon, I felt like a champion
(even though I didn't look like one).*

enter a lottery to get a slot. So, we did that, and as fate would have it, we got in!

The week before the marathon, Superstorm Sandy hit, and the flood waters it generated devastated much of the area, including Staten Island where the marathon starts. After several days of back and forth, and only three days before the marathon was supposed to occur, officials made the right call and canceled the race.

That left 40,000-plus runners with a decision to make: to run their own marathon or not run at all. I was fully trained and ready to go, so what was I going to do? I remember being on the phone with Kyle. He said, "Dave, it's your call. I will do whatever you want." I was about to pull the plug but decided to think about it a bit more. I told Kyle that I would call him back.

I sat silently for a while mulling over the whole thing. I told myself, "What's the point of going to the trouble if the race is not official?"

Then, I thought about my commitment. *I said I would run the New York City Marathon* and I realized I could still do it whether it was official or not. I called Kyle back and said, "F@% it! Let's do it!" Before we knew it, we were up at 6:00 a.m. and on our way to Central Park to do our own New York City Marathon. The best part was that we were not alone; there were thousands of other runners who had the same idea!

I thought about my commitment. I said I would run the marathon, and I realized I could still do it whether it was official or not.

We did a six-mile loop around Central Park, ran a few miles uptown to 125th Street, and then went down the West Side another 10 miles or so to the Brooklyn Bridge. From there, we ran through Brooklyn, where we met my wife at the entrance of Prospect Park. While my parents watched the kids, she ran the full loop with us. I was in pain and was going slow, but I finished and got to the end.

I again kept my commitment and ran the marathon! I felt great inside even though my outside was hurting. Since the official marathon had been canceled, anyone who had been registered for that year's marathon was automatically entered to run in it the following year. So, my marathon journey to keep my commitment to run the New York City event continued, but the next time it was alone, as Kyle had moved back to Ohio to continue his own journey. Read his book, *Follow the Dragons*, to learn more.

New York City Marathon #2 and the Staph Infection

The next year I was ready to finally run in the official New York City Marathon. However, as I started my first month of training, something unexpected happened: I cut my elbow, and soon it had doubled in size.

When I returned to the ER for a second time, I learned that staph infections can become deadly at the drop of a hat if they get into your bloodstream and go to your heart. It is a very serious thing because while you seem okay one minute, and the next you can be in a life-threatening situation. The doctor admitted me to the hospital and put me on intravenous antibiotics right away.

Over the next two days, the medical team administered multiple courses of IV antibiotics, but nothing seemed to slow the infection. Finally, the surgeon walked into my room and said, "We need to open up your elbow and clean it out. We cannot risk keeping this going for much longer." At 34 years old, it was my first stay in a hospital, and now I was going to have my first surgery. As they were about to put me to sleep with gas, I heard them counting backward and said, "That is so weird ... you guys sound funny."

The doctors looked at each other with puzzlement. "Why is he still ... oh wait ... turn that kn ... " and I was out.

They successfully cleaned out the infection and things got better, but changing the dressing of an open wound is a whole new level of pain. Morphine was my friend but did not do much.

Perhaps the worst thing was that the doctors said I could not train for at least a few weeks, if not longer. My parents heard that and tried to convince me to run the marathon another year.

I thought of Jack Canfield's story for Principle 54. "If my child's life was on the line, what would I do?" To me, if I could train, I was *going* to train and I was going to run in the marathon. Before I read this book, *before I truly realized the power of making a commitment and sticking to it,* I would have put the marathon off to the next year or maybe indefinitely. It was keeping this commitment that gave me the focus I needed to get through my marathon training.

Marathon Day

The day of the marathon was like a scene from a movie. It was the first such event after the terrible Boston Marathon bombing, and the police presence was like nothing I have ever seen in years past. Police helicopters were hovering around the start and throughout the race. It looked to me like there were military personnel everywhere. The area around the finish line also was surreal. What is normally a very crowded scene, with thousands of people cheering runners on, was dead silent. They had closed it off to everyone except for officials and those who ran the race.

The Finish Line

As I headed into Central Park, I was approaching mile 23 and I knew what was coming. This time I was without Kyle, and I was going to test my ability to break through the runner's wall that I had hit two years earlier in Philly. Through each mile after that point, I was in a world of pain and suffering, but the wall never truly came. I finished the marathon, and the photo of me smiling with a thumbs-up looked nothing like my near-death appearance at the Philadelphia finish line two years earlier (see the photo!).

The Power of Keeping Your Commitments

I made a big commitment to get in better shape by running the Philadelphia Marathon. Then I committed to run the New York City Marathon. Keeping these two agreements led me to run 750 miles over a three-year

I finished the New York City Marathon smiling and giving a thumbs-up!

period. As a result, I was able to transform myself from someone who only ran a 5K once to an experienced marathon runner.

From small commitments, such as attending a meeting, to large ones like running a marathon, if you keep your commitment as if your loved one's life is on the line, you will have that much more focus when facing a wall in front of you.

What happens too often in business and life is we hit a wall, and we don't have a clear vision of what we are trying to achieve, let alone a plan of attack. When we hit that wall, more often than not we stop, we turn around, we pivot. All this is part of gaining more experience.

Keeping your commitments is the key ingredient to staying outside your comfort zone longer. The number one way to keep your commitment is to have a plan to see it through. The simpler the plan the better, because you are more likely to both write it down and follow it. In Chapter 9, I share the main ingredients to include in your plan, whether you are running your marathon or growing your business.

9 CREATE A TRAINING PLAN

 *10 Minutes*

1. Use Milestones and Dates
2. Choose an Accountability Partner
3. Keep Track of Your Progress

o achieve your goals—to get out of your comfort zone and stay there—you need to create a training plan. Despite our best intentions, we often don't get around to planning because we're intimidated by it. We think it has to be more complicated than it really needs to be. This chapter will show how to keep planning simple so you actually DO IT!

1. Use Milestones and Dates

Achieving your goals based on passion alone usually isn't enough. There is a clear separation between those who operate on passion and those who follow a plan. Imagine it is your first time training for a marathon, but you decide to run only when you have time, and you are spitballing your mileage. You run long on weekends but shorter on weekdays. You have not thought ahead, and on the day of the marathon, you will find out how long you last. You *may* be fine, and you *may* complete the marathon, BUT it will certainly be much harder to stay mentally tough when you are tired. And when you hit that dreaded wall, it will be even tougher to believe that you can break through it.

That's why having a plan is so important. It helped me with running the marathon, and it most definitely will help you in your business and life.

The number one thing that got me to finish the race was that I knew the 16-week training program I had followed was time-tested. A key aspect of this kind of training program is that it has interim milestones. When I trained for the marathon, I had to run set mileage amounts on each date, and at the end of the week, I was able to know if I accomplished my goal.

WEEK	MON	TUE	WED	THU	FRI	SAT	SUN
1	CROSS	3 m run	5 m run	3 m run	Rest	5 m pace	10
2	CROSS	3 m run	5 m run	3 m run	Rest	5 m run	11
3	CROSS	3 m run	6 m run	3 m run	Rest	6 m pace	8
4	CROSS	3 m run	6 m run	3 m run	Rest	6 m pace	13
5	CROSS	3 m run	7 m run	3 m run	Rest	7 m run	14
6	CROSS	3 m run	7 m run	3 m run	Rest	7 m pace	10
7	CROSS	4 m run	8 m run	4 m run	Rest	8 m pace	16
8	CROSS	4 m run	8 m run	4 m run	Rest	8 m run	17
9	CROSS	4 m run	9 m run	4 m run	Rest	Rest	Half Marathon
10	CROSS	4 m run	9 m run	4 m run	Rest	9 m pace	19
11	CROSS	3 m run	10 m run	3 m run	Rest	10 m run	20
12	CROSS	3 m run	6 m run	3 m run	Rest	6 m pace	12
13	CROSS	3 m run	10 m run	3 m run	Rest	10 m pace	20
14	CROSS	3 m run	6 m run	3 m run	Rest	6 m run	12
15	CROSS	3 m run	10 m run	3 m run	Rest	10 m pace	20
16	CROSS	3 m run	8 m run	3 m run	Rest	4 m pace	12
17	CROSS	3 m run	6 m run	3 m run	Rest	4 m run	8
18	CROSS	3 m run	4 m run	Rest	Rest	2 m run	Marathon

Our marathon training plan helped Kyle and me keep our commitment.

Kyle and I committed to following the training program to a "T." (See the sample plan on the previous page.) We ran through what felt like monsoon rain and got soaked to the bone. We also ran on the hottest of days and had to keep stopping because we could not catch our breath. It was a challenge, but we did it!

Here's what I learned from the experience: *If you have a great training plan with a goal and dates that you are able to follow, it allows you to put all your mental energy into being fearless when walls appear in front of you.*

Planning at Lawline

Working with Mark Green in 2015, we created specific plans for one-year initiatives and three-month priorities. These included goals or outcomes attached to dates because, just like marathon training, a plan will not be effective unless you have milestones that you can easily track.

(By the way, attaching dates to goals is the hardest part of any plan. Why? Because it is at that moment when you are making your first real commitments. This is why many people skip this step. A line I like to repeat is "If your goals are not tied to dates, you are running on passion, not a plan.")

At Lawline, we put our priorities in writing and used a quarterly priority tool, provided by Mark Green, as shown on the next page. This was our version of a "training plan."

Thanks to Mark, it became clear to me that I had essentially been "winging it" all of the previous years when we didn't do real planning, and that was only going to take us so far. Back then, whenever I hit a wall without a clear vision of where I was going, all too often I would kill a priority (like TrueStartups).

Performance Dynamics Group ↗

🏛 Lawline Quarterly Priority Planning Tool

Objective: _____

Owner: _____ Team: _____

Why Is This Objective Important?

Key Results by Month

1.	
2.	
3.	

Clear Measure of Success

The Lawline Quarterly Priority Planning Tool

One of the things that Mark likes to say is "routine will set you free." And that it did. Over the next three years, we stayed consistent with our communication rhythms, strategy planning, and commitments to execute what we agreed to do.

Our planning at Lawline worked and I felt elated! By 2017, the executive team had been humming along for three years, and we had built a strong foundation for the company, thanks to the new focus that we lacked in the early years. I had broken the repetitive process of hiring and firing a COO every two years. In fact, I had decided to hold off on hiring a new COO entirely.

Success in this area came from a combination of keeping our commitments and having a business version of a marathon-training plan, both for the quarter and the year. That is what allowed us to keep *growing our comfort zone* and pushing the boundaries to stay outside of it, which in turn has allowed us to grow the company.

Staying Out of Our Comfort Zone—The Next COO Step

After almost three satisfying years of very productive planning and routine, I decided that it was once again time to shake up our current leadership structure so that we could get to the next level as a team and a business.

To be honest, a lot of the struggles I have had over the years as a leader and entrepreneur made me feel like there was something wrong with me. I didn't like holding people accountable. I had one idea after the other and would start one before I finished the other. I would think anything was simple and doable if I *just got started.* I did not sweat the important details and was always trying to be a big picture guy. The result, until Mark came aboard, was a company that was working on too many things at once without a clear direction of where we were heading.

Although I knew that the new processes we had been implementing were best for the company and the team, they often made me feel stifled. If I had new ideas or opportunities I wanted to pursue or share, I had to wait until the next planning cycle, either quarterly or annually, to fit them into our process. I found myself going off and doing things on my own, which worked out great until I was ready to integrate them and got blocked. It was a good thing, however; the company was now protected from my many ideas, which could make us lose focus.

The executive team was reporting to me in weekly coaching sessions. I was doing a decent job, but I knew I was stuck in helping them grow. I started to feel stifled in my creativity, as well as in my ability to help those under me break through their walls. On the plus side, the company's revenue engines were growing again at percentage levels we had not seen since the first few years.

I once again found myself on the phone with my mentor, Ben, sharing my struggles. After a few minutes of listening, he said, "It sounds like you have a classic visionary/integrator problem."

"A *what* problem?" I responded.

He went on, "There is a book called *Rocket Fuel*, authored by Gino Wickman and Mark Winters, that discusses why so many CEO-COO relationships fail and what to do about it. You are missing an integrator." Within a few minutes, he sent me a video (go to ffwdminset.com/resources) that overviewed the V/I dynamic in four minutes. I was sold and bought the book that night.

As it turns out, many founders of companies have traits similar to mine: They have a lot of ideas and want to share them all the time; however, they don't like the details or spending the time to hold people accountable. *Sound familiar?*

The classic V/I relationship was Walt and Roy Disney. Walt got all the credit for the ideas, but it was his brother Roy who managed the day-to-day activities, business or duties and filtered all of the ideas Walt had for Disney. A successful V/I relationship will enable the visionary to bring all of their creative ideas to the integrator, who then will help integrate those with the most powerful and timely fit for the company's needs. The integrator acts as the COO, managing the day-to-day activities, business or duties while also keeping the visionary up to date.

The key to creating a successful V/I relationship is finding the right match of personalities and skills. That is not easy, and as the book notes, often does not work on your first couple of attempts. (When I read that, it drove home the point that I was not alone in my past COO challenges.)

I knew right away what to do. Sigalle, who had approached me four years earlier to be COO, was not the right fit then, but at this particular point, she was exactly what the company needed. Over the years, she had instituted new systems and processes in each department she took on, allowing each team to grow. She had the respect of all her peers and, most importantly, we had great respect and admiration for each other.

On July 2, 2018, we launched the V/I concept at Lawline, promoting Sigalle to COO, and right away our growth started to accelerate. Why? Sigalle focused on growing our teams and processes while I put all my focus on growing the company as a whole.

As we added the V/I role, it also made sense to bring two new leaders onto the executive team. This allowed other team members throughout the company to grow beyond their roles as well. Now that we had a strong V/I relationship, a great executive team, and company culture built on focus and structure, we were poised for great things ahead!

2. Choose an Accountability Partner

If you really want to stick to a "training plan," you need an accountability partner—an individual or small team of people who will call you out on shortcuts and occasional bouts of laziness (hey, it's only human), while also acting as your cheerleaders. Kyle obviously served in this role for me when we ran the Philadelphia and New

York City Marathons. I put my trust in him to keep me on course—both literally and figuratively—and he came through each time.

In my professional life, Mark Green and Kim Ades have been among my most important accountability partners, monitoring results and ensuring that I was staying true to my goal and training plans. (Accountability benefits teams as well. Research shows that the peer-to-peer accountability created through team kickoffs can contribute to performance improvements by up to 30 percent!)

Having an accountability partner can often make for a symbiotic relationship—you can keep each other true to the plan, as my publisher Michael Roney and I did in developing this book. We put together a plan where we both had responsibilities and milestones over a set period of time, then checked in regularly with one another to confirm progress.

Those regular check-ins are critical. A study by the American Society of Training and Development (ASTD) found that you have a 65 percent chance of completing a goal if you simply commit to someone but a success rate of 95 percent if you have a specific accountability appointment with the person to whom you've committed!

The busier you are, the more you can probably use an accountability partner. As president of EO's New York City chapter, I am very busy in my day-to-day role. I am CEO of my own company. I am writing this book. I have a lot of irons in the fire, so to speak, and I need help to get everything done. That is why I bring in coaches and other experts to help me stay accountable with the required focus. Recently, I added growth consultant Bryan Wish to my book team, providing even more focus on spreading *The FFwd Mindset* message.

Over the years, I have hired and worked with experts who have been tremendous accountability buddies for me: Paulie Rojos on public speaking, Jamie Klein on HR, Bruce Eckfeldt on operations, and William Lieberman on my day-to-day finances. Our EO board's chapter manager, Beth Chernick, joins me on weekly calls to keep me focused on how we are doing with our yearly plan. You can add to this list Sigalle, my sister, of course my wife, and my parents.

Take a moment to write down a list of all the accountability buddies you have in your life. There are probably many more than you realize.

My Accountability Buddies

✓ Kim – thought management
✓ Mark – leadership
✓ Paulie – public speaking
✓ Michael – book
✓ Bryan – messaging
✓ Jamie – HR
✓ Bruce – Ops
✓ William – finances
✓ Beth – focus
✓ Sigalle
✓ Kelli
✓ Mom
✓ Dad

3. Keep Track of Your Progress

Creating interim milestones that allow you to monitor your training progress each day is not a strategy limited to business or running, of course. In fact, this practice was made famous by Jerry Seinfeld. His version goes like this:

You set a small daily goal for each day. (In Seinfeld's case, it was writing three jokes.) Get a calendar for the year and write an X on it every day that you reach your goal. The first day you write an X, then the next day you write another X, then do the same the following day, and so on. Before you know it, you're looking at two weeks of Xs! Pretty impressive, right?

Now, the number one thing you want to focus on is *not breaking that chain!!* Keep those Xs going as long as you can. Jerry did this every day, and in three months, he had written nearly 100 jokes! Try sitting down and doing that. If you build this into your daily routine, it could be virtually painless, and you're golden!

The beauty of this practice is that you can use it to build just about anything into your daily routine. Think of the one thing, the three things, that if done daily will get you to your goal. That's focus!

So many apps these days make it easy to not break the chain for things that will make you healthier or happier. For example, I am using an app called Seven which gamifies doing a daily seven-minute workout!

There are lots of other apps that offer the same thing. MyFitnessPal and Duolingo both provide daily reminders that help keep alive a streak of either entering the food you consume or learning Spanish. Timehop sends you a nudge to take a look at your photos and lets you know how many days in a row you viewed them.

I think these strategies are brilliant because they are a win-win. They get you to use the app more often, and at the same time help you create a daily, beneficial habit.

Tracking my daily marathon training progress is what pushed me to keep the streak alive as well. Not only would I write mileage, but I would share a little something about the run itself.

Staying Out of Your Comfort Zone Longer: FFwd Your Impact

Ultimately, you will be able to stay out of your comfort zone and stay focused longer by 1) creating a training plan with dates and goals, 2) choosing an accountability partner, and 3) keeping track of your progress. This is key to pushing through the walls that either you create because of a decision you make, or that come from an outside force. Staying out of your comfort zone is by definition uncomfortable. Use your plan as your North Star to get through it.

You will never create one as certain as a marathon-training plan because that has been repeatedly tested, refined, and proven for decades. You will, at times, choose the wrong goals or create time-frames that are too aggressive. That is great. Why? Because if you did not have a plan to begin with, you would have no idea of your *original* expectations going into it. If that happens, readjust, NIP fear in the Bud, and keep moving forward.

Creating long lasting impact takes focus!

I will repeat that again for both of our benefits. *Creating long lasting impact takes focus!*

To find that focus, you first need to take action. There is no doubt about this. Take action, and you absolutely will do more than those who stay in their comfort zones and remain frustrated with their lack of impact. I will take action any day of the week versus over-thinking about doing something but staying still. That is what Step 1 is about.

When you take action, it will lead to fear. Fear is a good thing. Fear protects you. Fear keeps you alert. Fear lets you know it is important. Your job is not to remove fear, but instead to NIP it in the Bud when it shows up! That is what Step 2 is all about. You do it in the moment. Its ugly head appears, so you NIP it, and you do not stop until it goes away!

Finally, you will reach Step 3, which is Find Your Focus! Treat your commitment as if your loved one's life is on the line. Create a simple training plan, team up with someone to hold you accountable, and keep track of your progress.

By combining all three steps, you will not only get out of your comfort zone, you will stay there longer. That is how you grow as an individual. If you want to have a larger impact on the world around you, you have to grow. There is no way around it.

In order to grow and stay out of your comfort zone longer, you need to put your focus in writing. The Step 3 Plan will allow you to put the key components of your "training plan" on a one-page document.

STEP **3** PLAN

FIND YOUR FOCUS

F inding *focus* is the number one ingredient for keeping yourself from falling back into your comfort zone after you take the leap of faith to go outside of it. It is very common for visionaries (which is the cloth most founders are made of) to get out of their comfort zone and do their best to NIP Fear in the Bud when they can. However, just like what happened with me and TrueStartups, without *focus* these visionaries would end up back in their comfort zones instead of breaking through their walls and having real impact.

Focus is dependent on an unrelenting, driving force *to keep your commitment* as if your loved one's life is on the line. That will help you get through the toughest walls that most "normal" people would not want to suffer through. And that is where the fundamentals of *planning* come into play. You need to have *clear goals with dates*, and you need to complete them in writing.

I have been guilty of writing out many plans without dates. That's because committing to those dates is the hardest part of all this. **Dates are when you change something from an idea to a commitment.**

Training Plan (Basic Overview):

The key is to include dates and times for when you are planning to get things done. Don't worry about following these to a "T." They are most important for seeing if you are actually doing what you were planning or are putting things off.

Accountability Partner(s):

Your accountability partner can be a coach or consultant that you hire, such as Kim, Mark, Michael, or Bryan. It can be a buddy that you run with, like Kyle. Or it can be a mentor, like Ben or your dad. Having accountability partners increases your chances of keeping your commitment. You need to meet with them regularly to keep tabs on your progress!

Your Victory Feeling (In past tense as if it already happened):

This is using the power discussed in Napoleon Hill's bestseller, *Think and Grow Rich*, along with Rhonda Byrne's *The Secret* and Gina Mollicone-Long's *Think or Sink*. It is the same thing I did with Kim in my first exercise with her. Act as if your goal has already happened and your mind will better focus on what it needs to do to make it happen.

30 Days to Keep Track

Like Jerry Seinfeld's joke-writing strategy (see Chapter 9), plan to do something small every day—something that will advance you toward your goal—and don't break the chain! Consider my marathon plan. Every single day for 120 days, I kept track of what I did. Regardless if I did something, nothing, or next to nothing, I put it on my tracker.

You need to do the same thing with your plan. Keep track of the number one thing you did each day to keep your agreement. Make sure you don't miss a day for the first 30 days.

After the first 30 days, rinse and repeat as much as you like. At that point, it is up to you to keep your commitment! (To download a template for this plan, visit ffwdmindset.com/resources.)

30 Days to Keep Track

SUNDAY	MONDAY	TUESDAY	WEDNESDAY	THURSDAY	FRIDAY	SATURDAY
		X 1	X 2	X 3	X 4	X 5
X 6	X 7	8	9	10	11	12
13	14	15	16	17	18	19
20	21	22	23	24	25	26
27	28	29	30	31		

STEP **3** PLAN

FIND YOUR FOCUS

Training Plan (Basic Overview)
Key: Attach dates & times to goals or outcomes.

30 DAYS
X each day you track
what you did.

1	2	3	4	5	6	7
8	9	10	11	12	13	14
15	16	17	18	19	20	21
22	23	24	25	26	27	28
29	30					

Your Victory Feeling
(In past tense—as if it has already
happened)

Accountability Partners

YOUR HERO'S JOURNEY

 *4 Minutes*

The hero's journey is cemented in our collective unconscious and is as old as humankind itself. The hero goes on an adventure, faces crises (walls), but overcomes them and is transformed into something greater than he or she ever was before, significantly impacting the surrounding world. As an entrepreneur, you are living your own hero's journey. You are building a business, daring to be different, and having an impact. Your personal growth is the essential part of this journey since (as Mark Green often notes) businesses never grow faster than their leaders.

During much of your journey, you *want* to be out of your comfort zone. That's because the longer you can stay out of your comfort zone, the faster you will grow. As with most heroes, traveling out of your comfort zone means you will face challenges, some bigger than others. Your success and growth all depend on how you react to those walls you face along your journey.

Heroic Guides

All heroes need guides and mentors to help them along their road—just like Yoda, Luke, Hagrid, Medea, Obi-Wan Kenobi, or any number of others who have played those roles in myth and literature. As entrepreneurs, we have many books and wise coaches to help guide us along the way. With this book, I am humbly assuming the role of one of your guides.

As a part of my service to you, I've included in this book some key wisdom from my own heroic author-guides like Jack Canfield and Dale Carnegie, as well as my in-person guides, Kim Ades, Mark Green, and yes, my dad. They and other great how-to business writers of yesterday and today can offer a deep well of insight and inspiration.

There is a lot of power in simplicity. Books that are successful and stick in the minds of their readers usually offer a very simple, actionable concept that changes the way you think, which over time leads to a behavior change.

That is the reason the book by Mel Robbins, *The 5 Second Rule*, has become so popular—because it's so simple. Mel offers this formula: when you do not want to do something, just count backward from 5, and when you reach 0, take some physical action—get up and do something! This simple concept prevents you from overthinking and allows you to take action.

Likewise, Hal Elrod's *The Miracle Morning* gives you three simple, easily repeatable steps for waking up an hour earlier each day so that you can focus on yourself. These transformed me from someone who would hit snooze over and over again into a "morning person." Hal's three-step process goes like this:

1. Put your alarm within walking distance from your bed.
2. When you get up to turn off the alarm, brush your teeth right away.
3. Then drink a full glass of water.

After that, you are officially up and ready to take on the world (assuming you went to sleep at a reasonable time).

Simon Sinek's best-selling book, *Start with Why*, drives home the point that all companies know *what* they do, and most know *how* they do it, but very few know WHY they do what they do. Simon gives you the formula to figure that out.

The E-Myth by Michael Gerber shares the concept that most business owners are not true entrepreneurs but employees stuck in their businesses. He points out that most entrepreneurs have moments of inspiration followed by years and years of tediously doing their "job." As an antidote, he suggests that you need to work *on* your business, not *in* it, and offers the tools that will allow you to do that.

The FFwd Mindset is a three-step formula to 1) Take Action, 2) NIP Fear in the Bud, and 3) Find Your Focus. It allows you to be more fearless and focused to accelerate your success and impact on the world around you.

Living the Hero's Journey

To live the hero's journey, you do not have to be a "superhero." In fact, entrepreneurship is quite the opposite. It is filled with doubt, fear, and indecision, to name just a few of the mental challenges we face. When you feel these things, it is because you have chosen to move out of your comfort zone, and that, of course, is good!

YES, you can get out of your comfort zone and not have the outcomes you want. YES, you will hit roadblocks and walls. YES, it will take a lot longer than you want. YES, you will have low moments. Just know that even Babe Ruth, the most famous slugger in baseball history, was also was known for a long time as the "King of Strikeouts."

Your success is not about how many home runs you hit; it has nothing to do with it. Your success is about how many times you walk up to the plate and swing the bat!

Use this book as your own heroic guide to be more *fearless* and *focused* when needed. Use the FFwd Mindset to get out of your comfort zone and stay there longer.

Use the stories in this book to remind yourself that you are *not alone* and that everything you are going through happens to many entrepreneurs. During my entrepreneur TV show interviews, I learned the number one factor for growth was *taking action*. It's as simple as that.

Start believing today! Take action!

EPILOGUE

 *2 Minutes*

My decision to write this book was a direct result of wanting to live my FFwd Mindset. It is also what led me to run for president of EO. It led me to create a keynote speech on this topic and speak to thousands of entrepreneurs on how to grow faster.

Living the FFwd Mindset led my family to make the decision to move to Barcelona for the 2019–2020 school year, so I could focus on expanding Lawline internationally, while at the same time giving my children an amazing experience that they would otherwise not get.

Living the FFwd Mindset is what led me to reach out to Acton Academy to start a middle school in Brooklyn (still in the idea stage). If I could take my entrepreneurship journey and wrap it up into a school, their model would be it. The kids live their own hero's journey just like we all do. They do not have teachers; they have guides. They don't have science fairs; they have business fairs. It is everything I dreamed of when I started TrueNYC 10 years ago.

Living the FFwd Mindset is why I am going to write 18 books over the next 10 years. It is why I am going to become a pilot by the time I am 50 (I am 41 at the time of this writing).

I will not label my results, regardless of whether they did or did not end up where I wanted them. I will be patient, with the goal of experiencing as much as I can with a FEARLESS FOCUS.

Below, you'll find my 2050 vision, stated in past tense as if it already has happened! If I look back in 30 years after spending my time trying to FFwd my impact in these areas, regardless of my results, I will have no regrets!

My 2050 Vision

By 2050 I have started, taken part in, and invested in entrepreneurial organizations that have had a significant impact in three areas:

1. Fast-Forwarding People's Impact:
Off of the success of the FFwd Mindset, I built several companies that provided mental tools and resources for millions of people that helped them grow as individuals and entrepreneurs.

2. Increasing Sustainability:
I started and took part in several companies that had a huge impact on the environment that drastically reduced the world's plastic footprint, significantly increased plant-based foods, and invested heavily in renewable energy.

3. Disrupting Education:
I was part of schools and organizations that properly prepared students for the innovation that was to come. In addition, we drastically reduced the cost of higher learning and made lifelong learning easily accessible for millions of people around the world.

Epilogue

So here's the question I want to leave you with: What vision of your own will you be able to look back on in 10, 20, or 30 years and know that you will have no regrets—regardless of the end results—by living your FFwd Mindset?

THE **FFwd Mindset**

PLAN

One of my favorite lines to say to my team is *"If it is not in writing, we are fighting."* When I trained for the marathons, I wrote plans to keep track of every single run I did and how far I went. Over the past four years at Lawline, I have written over a dozen priority plans, and as a team, we had close to a hundred plans written and executed. There is no question in my mind that these written plans allowed us to be that much more successful at staying focused and keeping our agreements. In fact, a 2007 study at the Dominican University of California found that the people with written goals were 42 percent more likely to achieve them.

While both the Lawline quarterly planning tool and my marathon training plan are good ways to enhance direction and focus on goals, including a granular look at what steps need to happen on given dates, they *do* lack one key component: they don't state in writing what can help you *build more confidence and overcome your fear.*

That is where this FFwd Mindset Plan comes in. As I was developing this, I was intent on making sure that it measured up to several requirements that I believe are necessary for it to create real impact for entrepreneurs:

1. It has to be simple enough so that even if you never read this book, or have any other instructions, you can fill it out and get value from it.

2. You can complete it in as little as five minutes.

3. You do not need to be able to complete the entire plan for it to add value for you.

4. You can fill out as many of these as needed for future goals.

5. You can use this plan to keep track of all the goals you complete.

6. The concept is memorable enough so that even if you forget all the details, you can do it in your head if needed.

The FFwd Mindset Plan is the Step 1, 2, and 3 plans combined into a one-page document. You can (but are not required to) fill out each individual step plan first, and then combine them all in shorthand to this one document. The process of writing each step out twice will help you finalize your thoughts.

Following is the FFwd Mindset Plan template and an example of how I completed mine for one of my goals: publishing this book! You can download unlimited templates of the FFwd Mindset Plan at ffwdmindset.com/resources.

The FFwd Mindset Plan

Date: _____

Step 1: Take Action

Where *do I want to be more FEARLESS or FOCUSed (e.g., complete a 26.2-mile marathon)?*

What *step out of my comfort zone is this (1–10)?*

Why *am I doing this?*

When *will I start?*

Step 2: NIP Fear in the Bud!

I am Not Alone in _____. I will get through it by Playing the Part as a Fearless _____.

My #1 Fear:

Not Alone *(Who else is going through this?)*:

I Will Get Through It *(Past experience shows I have what it takes.)*:

Play the Part *(Why I am FEARLESS and do not care about what others think.)*:

Step 3: Find Your Focus

My Training Plan *(Basic overview in a sentence or two.)*:

Accountability Partner(s) *(Who will make sure you stick to your plan?)*:

My Victory Feeling *(In past tense as if it already happened.)*:

The First 30 Days *(Keep a day-by-day log or journal of how you are sticking to your plan.)*:

Keep Track of First 30 Days

Month 1

1
2
3
4
5
6
7
8
9
10
11
12
13
14
15
16
17
18
19
20
21
22
23
24
25
26
27
28
29
30

THE **FFWD** MINDSET PLAN

Title	Date	Please combine Steps 1, 2, & 3 Plans on this page

STEP 1 Take Action	Where?	Why?
	What comfort level?	When?

STEP 2 NIP Fear in the Bud	My #1 fear	I will get through it (Past Experience)
	Not alone	Play the part

STEP 3 Find Your Focus	My training plan	My victory feeling

Accountability partner(s)	First 30 (X each day you track)

1	2	3	4	5	6	7	8	9	10
11	12	13	14	15	16	17	18	19	20
21	22	23	24	25	26	27	28	29	30

THE **FFWD** MINDSET PLAN

Title **Publishing My Book**	Date	Please combine Steps 1, 2, & 3 Plans on this page

STEP 1
Take Action

Where?

Where do I want to be more FEARLESS or FOCUSed (e.g., complete a 26.2-mile marathon)? Publish my first book on entrepreneurship.

Why?

Why am I doing this? I am a Self-Help Addict (SHA). I get so much energy from books and they have had such an impact on my life that writing one has become an extension of that process. I am addicted to sharing knowledge that I have gained over the years to help others get to where they want to be faster. It is about no regrets and giving it your all.

What comfort level?

7

When?

When will I start?
Immediately, and I will target book release for MAY, 2019.

STEP 2
NIP Fear in the Bud

My #1 fear

My #1 Fear: When the book is released it will not be good, no one will read it, and it will just fade away. Or maybe I will never finish the book.

I will get through it (Past Experience)

I have done many challenging things over my life, from building my business, to running marathons, to being a father of three. I choose to go and do something HARD and face it head-on vs NOT. I had an entrepreneur TV show in law school as my commitment to sharing and teaching entrepreneurship and this book is a necessary next extension of that.

Not alone

There are 10,000 business books completed each year, and each author who has written a crappy book and a great book has had this feeling. It is part of the process. If the book is crap, then it will be crap and I will have hit my initial goal to publish the book. There is a famous quote: "I never told the world I would write a best-selling book, I just told the world that I would publish a book."

Play the part

I will not be concerned about what others think about the BOOK. The book is for ME first and all those critics in my head second. In fact, the critics that I keep hearing in my head are not the target market for the book. I am an amazing author who is going to have a big impact on those who want to grow themselves and their businesses.

STEP 3
Find Your Focus

My training plan

I will finalize draft one by November 30, get it to Michael, and get version two completed by year-end. Finally, version three will be completed by February 15, with a book release planned for early April. If needed, we will keep going back and forth until we feel the draft is the final version.

My victory feeling

I published my first book. This has been a lifelong dream. I am proud. Accomplished. I now have the basis for the next stage of my career. It will be the launching guide for a platform of entrepreneur impact I plan to have over the next 20 years.

Accountability partner(s)

Michael, Paulie, Kyle, Bryan.

First 30

X	X	X	4	X	X	7	X	X	10
1	2	3	4	5	6	7	8	9	10
1	2	3	4	5	6	7	8	9	10

30-Day CHALLENGE

On Day 1 you will create your FFwd Mindset Plan (page 149). From Day 2 to 30, you will KEEP TRACK and answer these three questions each morning in an online or physical journal.***

As it relates to your FFwd Mindset Plan:

Question 1: Actions from Yesterday?

Question 2: #1 Fear(s)?

Question 3: Focus for Today?

*Penzu is a free online journal software you can use for this challenge.
**After you reach 30 days, it is your choice to you continue. Or feel free to create an additional FFwd Mindset Plan and start a new 30-Day Challenge. It gets addicting. Good luck!
***I recommend finding an accountability partner to whom you can email this each day. For example, for my book launch plan, I emailed Bryan Wish my daily updates.

ACKNOWLEDGMENTS

I knew that writing this book was going to be one of the hardest things I have ever done, and I was right. The mental workout was much tougher than I could have anticipated. That just makes finishing it so much more meaningful. I, of course, could not have done it without a team supporting me along the way.

Any great book needs a great publisher to help the author throughout their journey. Michael Roney provided that guidance for over two years. Together we went through multiple iterations of *The FFwd Mindset* until I felt it was ready for prime time. The back and forth we had was constant and all-consuming at times. Regardless of my mood or what I said, Michael would always smile and work with me to make the changes. At the end of the day, that led to a book that is authentic to my voice, and the vision I had for this project. Thanks also to Highpoint's Sarah Clarehart, who took our input and skillfully produced the book's interior design and illustrations.

Meeting Bryan Wish came at just the right time, as I was looking for someone to help me market the book and spread the message. When we first started working together, that was his focus, but before I knew it, he had also rolled up his sleeves and was giving great substantive feedback on each chapter along the way. I have learned a large amount from him in a short time.

Creating the cover became a nightmare for those around me, as I sent version after version to my friends and family. All along the way, Damian Makki was patient and caring, always smiling with each new fix or change I had, and saying "not a problem—let's try it." I met him when he was a designer at Lawline, so it was fitting to have him design my cover years later.

I mentioned many people in this book who have touched and transformed my life. Kyle Robinson has always been one of the most caring and giving people I know. He set off on a journey in his life, and then he graciously shared it with the world in his book, *Follow the Dragons*. I am thankful to him for always being there for moral support and to share the meaning of life with me.

Meeting Kim Ades in 2012 changed my life for the better. She is an amazing coach who challenged me to grow as an individual and a leader. I told her that someday I would write a book from my journals, and I am so happy I kept that commitment! Her guidance as a coach, and now as a friend, is so important to me, and it will continue to be as we do great things together in the future.

Mark Green's guidance has been instrumental in my growth as a leader. He came to help our business at a challenging and pivotal time to provide just the right structure and focus I needed. His no-nonsense approach gave me the accountability required to push myself to the next level. I have been honored to be able to work with him over the years, and look forward to continued growth together as we both explore our author roots.

I am so thankful to Paulie Rojas for her weekly public speaking coaching as I prepared for several keynote speeches on The FFwd Mindset. Her guidance and support has been invaluable to making me a more dynamic and well-versed speaker. In 2014, Ben Kirshner became my peer mentor in Entrepreneurs Organization. His one requirement to mentoring me was that I keep my commitments, and I did! I am grateful for Ben's friendship, as following his advice over the years has been instrumental in my personal and my company's growth.

Sigalle Barness and Richard Hernandez were the first members, along with my sister, Michele Richman, on the Lawline executive team. They have made me a better person and leader in so many ways. Their passion for living a full life on every level has been so inspiring. Many thanks to them for their leadership over the years at Lawline and support for me as CEO.

I am thankful to everyone at Lawline who has supported my personal and professional growth. Two people mentioned in the book's stories are Jeff Reekers, who challenged me as COO, and who I love watching grow in his career. Also, Joe Tannenbaum, who made such a difference at Lawline, especially when he led the charge for building the new website.

I have also been blessed with many friends and family who have each been a rock for me during this book project. My long walks with Ari Raivetz at the farm, discussing the book and its progress, kept me going each year. Thanks also to my friend since kindergarten, David Shabsels, for always being a sounding board for my ideas whenever I needed it; Rachel Spiegelman, for diving deep into the concepts and helping me with my messaging; Jennifer Morris for always listening, and helping me figure out a "big stuck" on our icy walk with the kids to the waterfall.

How many people can say they have been working with their sister for the past 10 years? I know that in itself is special, but our connection goes so much deeper. Michele and I strive to challenge ourselves to grow as people and as professionals. We are there for each other when there is a family or business issue. We are also there to bicker and fight as a healthy brother/sister relationship should. I am so grateful to have her in my life, and I hope I challenge her growth as much as she challenges mine. And whenever I go too far, I am thankful to my brother-in-law David for making things smooth again.

My dad, Alan, has been with me through thick and thin over the years, as is a dad's job. His attitude is the exact type of guidance a son needs when he is trying to grow his business and fast-forward his impact. Our 90-mile hiking trip in Patagonia in 2017 is a memory that I will cherish for the rest of my life. I'm looking forward to our next adventure together (with Kelli's permission).

My mom, Judy, stepped up big time, reviewing draft after draft, giving me great feedback and editing. Our muscle memory came back quickly when we would work "together" during high school to finish my papers. She has a true knack for what sounds good, and I know I got my love for storytelling from her. I am lucky to have her in my life, always putting the family first.

My nephews, Max and Eli, were there for me, reviewing cover after cover and giving valuable feedback. My brother-in-law Ari Kalimi, a.k.a. DJ Affect, and his amazing wife, Jenny, showed up big time to help me with design and marketing ideas to get the book the attention it deserves. I also want to thank my mother-in-law, Randi, for just being the coolest cat in town, and my father-in-law, Sami, for being the biggest mench I know.

Finally, I want to thank my kids, Leila, Joshua and Jonah, for their patience. The most common phrase to be heard at night while I was typing away was "Are you still writing that book?" They have helped me out at all stages of the writing process, and I was always so happy to have their input. I am thankful for all the love and care Sandra has given the kids and our family over the years; I truly appreciate all her support. And I have saved the best for last. I want to thank my wife, Kelli, for being my best friend, my partner, my coach, my mentor, my everything. I could not have gotten through this without her support and guidance.

ABOUT THE AUTHOR

David **Schnurman** is the CEO of Lawline, the leading provider of online continuing legal education (CLE) in the country, serving over 130,000 attorneys with over three million courses completed. David is also the current president of Entrepreneurs Organization New York (2018-2019), a global association with members in 57 countries.

He is the recipient of the EO Rockies Award for Resourcefulness, a Fastcase 50 winner and a finalist for SmartCEO's Deals of Distinction Award. David is a frequent speaker to business organizations, colleges, and high schools on topics ranging from entrepreneurship, mindset, leadership, and culture, and has published articles on these topics in Forbes. His success has been recognized by his peers in entrepreneurship and the legal industry, and has been featured in The Wall Street Journal, Inc. Magazine, Entrepreneur.com, Crain's NY, the New York Post, and Law.com.

Lastly, David has a love for adventure and discovery. He has run several marathons. He has hiked the mountains of Patagonia, paraglided in Colorado, gone skydiving, and taken flying lessons. He currently lives in Brooklyn with his wife Kelli and three beautiful children.

INDEX

Note: Page numbers in *italic* indicate figures; page numbers in **bold** indicate tables.

CPSIA information can be obtained
at www.ICGtesting.com
Printed in the USA
BVHW04082608051
547713BV00012B/108/P

9 781645 708797